GROWING
FRUITS

NATURE'S
DESSERTS

June 1996

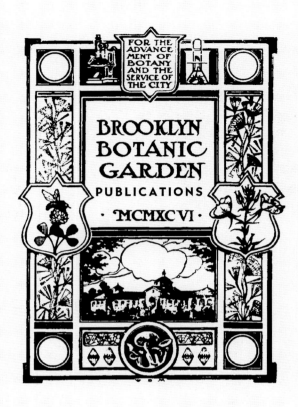

FOR THE
ADVANCE
MENT OF
BOTANY
AND THE
SERVICE OF
THE CITY

BROOKLYN
BOTANIC
GARDEN
PUBLICATIONS
· MCMXCVI ·

GROWING FRUITS

NATURE'S DESSERTS

Lee Reich - Guest Editor

Handbook #147

Copyright © Summer 1996 by the Brooklyn Botanic Garden, Inc.

Handbooks in the 21st-Century Gardening Series, formerly Plants & Gardens,

are published quarterly at 1000 Washington Ave., Brooklyn, NY 11225.

Subscription included in Brooklyn Botanic Garden subscribing membership dues ($35.00 per year).

ISSN # 0362-5850 ISBN # 0-945352-93-X

Printed by Science Press, a division of the Mack Printing Group

Table of Contents

INTRODUCTION
Sweet Rewards

BY LEE REICH

THE CRISPNESS OF THE AUTUMN APPLE, the buttery smoothness of the persimmon, the mellow flavor of a ripe blueberry or pear and the piquant flavor of a currant or strawberry.... Just think of the range in textures and flavors of fruits, Mother Nature's original desserts.

Full flavor in any fruit is achieved only when that fruit is grown well, then harvested at the right moment—and the way to experience that rich flavor is to grow the fruit yourself. Although commercial fruits must be picked while they're still underripe to be firm enough to survive the rigors of shipping and storage, plums you grow yourself can hang on the tree until they're bursting with ambrosial juice. And no need to pluck that blackberry until its final moments of ripening, when a mere touch stains your fingers. Fortunately, such blackberries need travel no farther than arm's length—to your mouth.

Planting your own fruit trees and bushes is an expression of freedom, the freedom to choose, for example, which from among the 5,000 or so varieties of apples suits your fancy. There's a slew of fruit varieties, even kinds of fruits, that you rarely, if ever, find in markets. What Liberty Hyde Bailey, the doyen of American horticulture, wrote almost 100 years ago about apples could apply equally well to all fruits: "Why do we need so many different kinds of apples?

You can harvest peaches and red raspberries—or any other fruits you grow yourself—from the plant just when they are bursting with ambrosial juices.

As a backyard fruit grower, you might not plant an orchard, but perhaps just a currant hedge, a grape arbor, a stately cherry or a stunning espaliered apple tree.

Because there are so many different kinds of folks. A person has a right to gratify his legitimate tastes. If he wants 20 or 40 kinds of apples for his personal use, running from 'Early Harvest' to 'Roxbury Russet', he should be afforded the privilege....There is merit in variety itself. It provides more points of contact with life, and leads away from uniformity and monotony."

Fruit growing in America underwent a dramatic change just after the middle of the 19th century. More Americans began planting the best European varieties of apples, peaches and pears, rather than relying on seedling trees whose fruits were fit only to feed hogs or to ferment into beverages. At the same time, interest developed in American varieties of these traditional European fruits—apple varieties such as 'Esopus Spitzenberg', 'Newtown Pippin' and 'Winesap', for example—as well as in native American fruits such as persimmons, pawpaws and juneberries.

I believe that we are now entering a new era in fruit growing, an era fueled by the desire for old-fashioned flavor and the joy of cultivating plants. Many people also grow their own fruits to limit the amount of pesticides in their foods, which is possible with backyard fruits because those that you grow yourself need not meet the stringent cosmetic standards demanded in commercial markets.

This handbook is for you, the backyard fruit grower, who might not plant an orchard, but might have just one row of dwarf fruit trees, perhaps a currant hedge enclosing the vegetable garden, a grape vine clambering up an arbor to shade a terrace or a stately cherry tree in the lawn.

Within these pages, you will find enough information to get you started in growing fruits of temperate zones or to expand your horizons—in knowledge or plants. Individual chapters are not meant to be encyclopedic, but rather to reflect the enthusiasm and biases of the authors, all of whom have extensive experience with the fruits about which they write.

Fruit growing can be a challenge, but if you plan ahead and then closely observe your plants as they grow, the challenge can be rewarding, both to your mind and your tongue. After a quarter century of studying and growing fruits, I am still making "adjustments" to my fruit garden, digging up plants whose fruits did not meet my expectations or that I overplanted, and setting promising new plants in their places. When my garden has yielded an overabundance of fruits, I am reminded of the words of Andrew Marvell, written over 300 years ago:

> What wondrous life is this I lead!
> Ripe apples drop about my head;
> The luscious clusters of the vine
> Upon my mouth do crush their wine;
> The nectarine and exquisite peach
> Into my hands themselves do reach;
> Stumbling on melons as I pass,
> Ensnared with flowers, I fall on grass.

Overabundance has been the result of poor planning on my part; but what a sweet learning experience.

Fruit Garden Basics

BY LEE REICH

IF YOU PLAN YOUR fruit garden carefully, and tailor your plant selections to your site and needs, you'll find growing fruits rewarding and enjoyable. The first and most important rule in garden planning is to choose fruits you love to eat. But don't be afraid to experiment and try new varieties of familiar and unfamiliar fruits. No matter what you grow, you will be pleased with the different—and superior—flavor of home-grown fruits.

POLLINATION

Once you've made a list of the fruits you'd like to grow, find out whether they require "cross-pollination," or fertilization with pollen from a different plant of the same species

Left: If you love apricots, make sure to plant one—and any other fruits you love to eat—in your garden.
Above: Find out if your choices require "cross-pollination" or are "self-fruitful."

in order to produce fruit. If you have chosen a fruit that needs cross-pollination, but lack space for two plants, don't despair: your neighbor might be growing a suitable pollinator, or you could put a pollinating bouquet, kept fresh in a bucket of water, near your plant—or you even could graft a single pollinator branch onto your plant.

Plants that do not need cross-pollination are "self-fruitful" (sometimes called "self-fertile"), and can fruit in isolation. Some plants will even bear fruit without any pollination whatsoever—either with their own pollen or that of another plant. As with self-fruitful plants, you can grow just one of these plants, and their fruits will be seedless.

SPACING AND YIELDS

The next factors to consider are how much of each fruit you will want to eat and how the plants fit into your garden. Plants need adequate spacing not only to make harvest easier, but because crowded branches tend to get less light, water or nutrients. The accompanying chart lists, for various fruits, planting distances and approximate yields of mature plants. Note that dwarf trees listed bear full-sized fruits.

SITE AND SOIL

For all their differences in geographical and botanical origins, fruit plants are remarkably similar in their site and soil needs. The ideal site for

SPACING & YIELDS

	SPACING (FT.)	YIELD (LBS.)
APPLE		
Dwarf	7	60
Semi-dwarf	12	150
Standard	20	300
APRICOT	15	150
BLACKBERRY		
Trailing	10	3
Erect, semi-erect	5	3
BLUEBERRY		
Highbush	5	7
Lowbush	2	1
Rabbiteye	8	15
CHERRY		
Sweet	25	300
Tart	10	100
CURRANT	6	8
GOOSEBERRY	5	8
GRAPE	8	15
JUNEBERRY		
Bushes	6	20
Trees	15	100
KIWI	8	150
NECTARINE	15	100
PAWPAW	15	50
PEACH	15	150
PEAR		
Dwarf	8	60
Standard	15	300
PERSIMMON	15	200
PLUM	10	75
RASPBERRY	2	3
STRAWBERRY	1	2

Semi-dwarf apple trees are smaller than full-sized trees, but with a yield of 150 pounds of fruit each season, may be just as much apple tree as you need. Growers create semi-dwarf trees by grafting the fruiting part of the plant, the scion (such as 'Mercer', above), onto a semi-dwarf rootstock.

most fruits is bathed in gentle, drying breezes and full sunlight (at least six hours per day of direct summer sun), and offers some shelter from frigid winter winds. Avoid low-lying areas, where cold air collects in spring and can subject early blossoms to killing frosts.

Don't let a less-than-ideal site discourage you from growing fruit, though. If your site is adequate but not perfect, you should still reap some harvest, albeit a smaller one. Tailor the fruits that you plan to grow to the microclimates in your yard. You might plant late-blooming medlars in that frost pocket, for instance, heat-loving peaches against a south wall, or shade-tolerant currants in the dappled light beneath a locust tree.

Wherever your site, you can alter the soil itself to suit fruit plants. Most of them thrive in a well-drained soil that is rich in humus and moderately fertile. Your first consideration is adequate drainage, which you can determine by digging a test hole and filling it with water. If your soil drains well, the water will be gone within 12 hours. If the soil is poorly drained, install ditches or underground perforated pipe to carry water off to a lower location, or else plant your fruits atop wide mounds of soil.

Abundant amounts of organic materials, such as compost and rotted leaves, hasten drainage in clay soils if mixed into the top 12 inches. While digging the soil, also mix in ground limestone or sulfur to raise or lower the soil pH, if needed.

In fact, organic materials are beneficial for all soils. They keep soil biologically active, hold moisture and air and buffer acidity. Once you have planted, continue to enrich the soil with organic materials by laying them on the surface as mulches. Mulches protect roots from hot sun, slow evaporation of water and smother weeds; leaching and earthworm activity gradually work these materials down through the soil. Replenish mulch whenever bare ground is beginning to show.

For many fruit plants, the mulch, especially if it is a nutrient-rich material such as straw-rich manure, provides all the nutrients needed. But keep an eye on growth. If leaves lack a vibrant green color or show burning at their edges, supplemental fertilizer might be necessary. Nitrogen is the most evanescent of soil nutrients, and a general rule is to spread 0.2 pounds per 100 square feet (the same area as the spread of the plant's leafy canopy). The actual amount of fertilizer to use depends on the percentage of nitrogen it contains, so if you have a fertilizer that contains 7 percent nitrogen, use it at the rate of three pounds (0.2 pounds divided by .07) per 100 square feet.

14

TRAINING AND PRUNING

Annual pruning is a must for most fruit trees, bushes and vines, beginning right when they are planted, so that the plant's branches are always bathed in sun and air and are sturdy enough to support bountiful yields.

Fruit trees are trained to one of two basic forms. The *central-leader* tree is shaped like a Christmas tree, with a single main stem—the central leader—off which grow progressively shorter scaffold limbs. The *open-center* tree is shaped like a vase, with three or four scaffold limbs growing upward and outward atop a short trunk.

A nursery tree is usually sold as a "whip," which is just a single stem, or as a "feathered tree," which is a single stem with side branches. Right after planting, cut back the whip by a quarter to a third to stimulate growth of side branches, some of which will become scaffold limbs. As the tree grows, select as scaffold limbs the basic structural branches of the tree, side branches that originate in a spiral fashion around the leader and are at least six inches apart. Remove all other growth as soon as you notice it. If there is a wide angle between a scaffold

PRUNING A WHIP & A FEATHER TREE

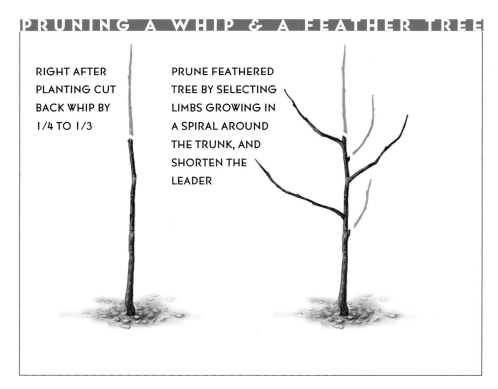

RIGHT AFTER PLANTING CUT BACK WHIP BY 1/4 TO 1/3

PRUNE FEATHERED TREE BY SELECTING LIMBS GROWING IN A SPIRAL AROUND THE TRUNK, AND SHORTEN THE LEADER

PRUNING A CENTER LEADER TREE

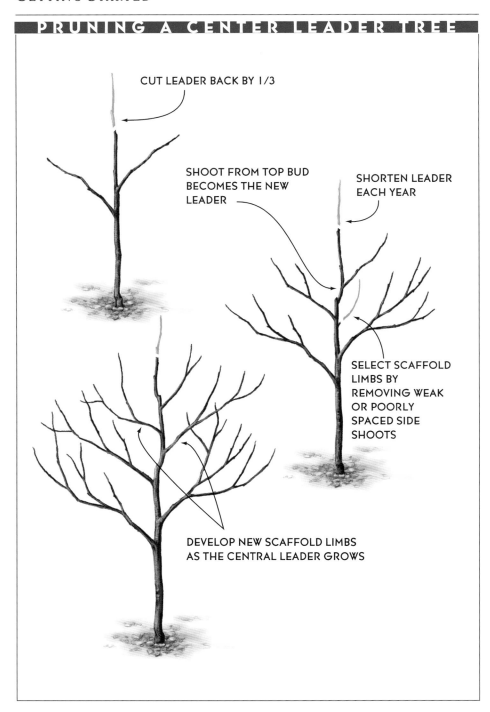

CUT LEADER BACK BY 1/3

SHOOT FROM TOP BUD BECOMES THE NEW LEADER

SHORTEN LEADER EACH YEAR

SELECT SCAFFOLD LIMBS BY REMOVING WEAK OR POORLY SPACED SIDE SHOOTS

DEVELOP NEW SCAFFOLD LIMBS AS THE CENTRAL LEADER GROWS

PRUNING AN OPEN-CENTER TREE

SELECT 3 OR 4 SCAFFOLD LIMBS,
REMOVE OTHERS

AFTER A SEASON'S GROWTH,
CUT SCAFFOLD LIMBS
BACK TO PROMOTE BRANCHING

IN SUBSEQUENT YEARS, REMOVE
SHOOTS THAT ARE TOO CLOSE TO
TRUNK AND SHORTEN LIMBS YOU
WISH TO ENCOURAGE TO BRANCH

PRUNING VINES

TRAIN VINE TO HAVE A PERMANENT
TRUNK—CUT BACK ALL STEMS
EXCEPT THE STURDIEST ONE

PINCH BACK ANY SIDE SHOOTS
EXCEPT THOSE THAT WILL BE
FRUITING ARMS OR CORDONS

TIE STEMS AND CORDONS TO A SUPPORT

These apple trees are espaliered, or trained flat against a support, creating a decorative hedge. Espaliering is a special method of pruning that makes trees as fruitful as they are decorative.

limb and the leader, the attachment between the two will be stronger, so select wide-angled scaffolds. You can also widen the angle by weighing down the scaffold branch or by wedging a piece of wood between the limb and the leader. The feathered tree already has side branches, so save ones that meet the above criteria and remove the rest.

After this initial shaping of the tree, your pruning technique will depend on the form of tree you desire. In the central-leader tree, growth from the top bud becomes a continuation of the central leader. In subsequent seasons, shorten the leader, as if it were a whip, to keep new scaffold limbs developing and the central leader growing. Choose three or four vigorous limbs as main scaffold branches for an open-center tree, then shorten each of them after a season of growth in order to get them to branch. In subsequent seasons, remove any branches crowding too close to the trunk along a scaffold branch, and shorten any limbs that you want to branch more.

Train a fruiting vine to have a permanent trunk and, perhaps, one or more permanent horizontal extensions called cordons. Temporary fruiting arms grow

To maximize the fruiting potential of your tree, make sure you don't create too much vertical growth, as above. Vertically trained branches will grow leaves, not fruit.

off the trunk or the cordon(s). When you plant, begin developing the trunk by cutting back all stems except the sturdiest one. Tie the stem as it grows to some sort of support, pinching back any side shoots that attempt to grow along its length or from the ground, except, of course, side shoots destined to become either fruiting arms or cordons.

Fruit bushes do not need training because none of their stems are permanent; over the years they are renewed by young sprouts from ground level.

As fruit plants—trees, vines or shrubs—attain maturity, prune them each year in order to keep them within bounds and open to light and air, to thin out excess fruits and to stimulate enough new growth for the coming season's fruit. Tailor your pruning to suit the growth and fruiting habit of each plant.

TEN STEPS TO
Pest-Free Fruits

BY SALLY ROTH

NOT SO VERY LONG AGO, managing pests and diseases was a matter of war. Total control was the only option. The only good bug, it seemed, was a dead bug. Some commercial orchards still follow this policy of overkill, but in home fruit gardens and in more and more commercial orchards, pest *management* has become the byword. Gardeners and growers have learned that so-called pests are a natural part of a garden. In the natural system, predators and weather help keep these insects in a balance we can live with.

Instead of spraying willy-nilly, savvy gardeners are learning to monitor pest levels and respond to problems with a calculated level of intervention. The presence of a few aphids on your pear tree, for

Shopping for disease-resistant fruit varieties like this apple, 'Liberty', is one of the best ways to keep your fruit garden pest-free.

This sticky ant barrier works by keeping climbing pests away from the fruit tree's blossoms and fruits.

instance, is no cause for panic. Chances are that ladybugs and other predators will make a meal of them long before they cause significant damage. No sense rolling out the big guns when a snip of the pruners can take care of the problem.

Using natural and mechanical controls, and following up only when necessary with chemical controls, is the basis of Integrated Pest Management (IPM). IPM calls for a bigger commitment from you, the gardener. You'll need to find out what the most common problems are in your area and start off with resistant stock. You'll have to keep a close eye on your fruit plants and trees. And you'll need to make decisions all along the way, about when to step in and what to use.

But we gardeners are already committed to spending time in the garden. Most of us start the morning and end the evening with a stroll through our gardens. We're quick to notice any unusual symptoms—a curled leaf, a blackened twig, a wilted flower.

❶ The IPM approach starts with shopping smart. Before you fill out that catalog order form, take a few minutes to talk to your county extension agent and speak to other gardeners. Pest problems vary from one area to another, so find out what pests are problems with the fruit you want to plant. Cedar apple rust can cause havoc on apples in the Northeast, but rarely rears its head in the West. Some pest problems are

COMMON FRUIT PESTS

APPLES AND PEARS

aphids
apple maggot
apple scab
cedar rust
codling moth
fire blight
mildew
plum curculio

STONE FRUITS

bacterial spot
brown rot
cherry leaf spot
Oriental fruit moth
peach scab
peach twig borers
plum curculio
powdery mildew
scales

BLUEBERRIES

botrytis tip blight
mummyberry
stem canker
stunt virus

STRAWBERRIES

anthracnose
aphids
gray mold
grubs
leather rot
mites
plant bug
red stele
sap beetles
verticillium wilt
weevil larvae

BRAMBLE FRUITS

anthracnose
cane blight
leaf curl
orange rust
phytophthora root rot
powdery mildew
raspberry mosaic
spur blight
verticillium wilt

GRAPES

anthracnose
black rot
botrytis bunch rot
crown gall
dead-arm
downy mildew
phylloxera
Pierce's disease
powdery mildew

widespread; others are limited to certain areas or growing conditions.

❷ Once you know what pests are prevalent in your area, you can seek out resistant varieties. You should have little trouble finding varieties that fight off viral, fungal and bacterial diseases, but most varieties of a fruit are usually equally susceptible to insect attack.

❸ Be sure to select plants that will thrive in your growing conditions. If your spring weather swings from warm back to cold, for example, look for varieties that are late to blossom, so that the flowers won't be damaged by frost. It's much easier to start out with well-adapted plants than it is to try to change your conditions to suit them. Plants not suited to your climate or conditions will be weakened by stress, and become more vulnerable to pests. You can kill your fruit trees with kindness, too: Too much fertilizer makes for overly succulent greenery, which is like a banquet sign to insect pests.

Gardeners have long relied on horticultural oils to control insects and mites. These refined petroleum oils work by plugging the orifices through which pests breathe.

❹ Learning when to step in is the basis of the IPM method. It's healthier for you and your plants if you learn to tolerate a certain amount of damage to your plants, and a few blemishes on your fruits. Avoid jumping in with too much pesticide, or too soon, so that the beneficial insects in your garden will have a chance to even the balance themselves.

❺ "Mechanical controls" are another vital part of the IPM approach. You are already employing mechanical controls if you tap off Japanese beetles from your grapevine into a jar of soapy water. Hand-picking is an excellent way to get rid of pests. A weekly once-over is often all that's needed. Other devices that fall into the mechanical controls category include sticky traps and pheromone traps, which attract and collect pests, chicken-wire bark scrubbers, which remove loose bark from tree trunks—a hiding place for eggs and overwintering insects—and cardboard barriers, which when wrapped around a tree trunk create a roadblock in the path of climbing pests. These simple devices are a great help in keeping pest populations at a low level. Your hose nozzle can be a good anti-pest device, too. Use it to

Microbial pesticides such as *Bacillus thuringiensis (Bt)*, and other bacterial and fungal pest controls are toxic to insect pests once ingested. *Bt*, a selective biocide, destroys the gut of many types of caterpillars.

blast off aphids and other insects. Sometimes the fastest way to get rid of a problem is to snip it off. If scale or aphids are heavily infesting a twig, cut off and destroy that twig for a quick remedy. Bagging fruit is often effective in keeping insects, diseases—even birds— at bay.

❻ Good housekeeping plays an important role in preventing pest problems. Put your pruners to use when you see signs of scorched, wilting leaves and twigs (the symptoms of fire blight) or cankers on stems. Cut off the affected parts, slicing back several inches into healthy wood. Carry a bucket of 10 percent bleach solution, and dip your pruners into it after each cut. Pick up or rake up dropped fruit and plant debris so that spores and insects don't overwinter.

❼ Indiscriminate use of pesticides kills off the many beneficial and harmless organisms in your garden, along with the pests. Try non-chemical controls before you turn to chemicals. Encourage beneficial wasps and other insects by planting patches of yarrow, oregano, mint, dill or other plants with abundant tiny flowers that supply nectar to these insect allies. Many gardeners release green lacewings,

Left: Many insects are sensitive to the rapid, damaging effects of insecticidal soaps.

Right: Botanical pesticides are derived from plants, and although they break down fairly rapidly when exposed to light, heat or water, they can be quite poisonous to pests—and people.

ladybugs, parasitic ichneumon wasps and other beneficial insects to boost natural populations, as well as packaged *Bacillus thuringiensis* (Bt), a bacteria that kills leaf-eating caterpillars.

⑧ Horticultural soaps and oils are another weapon in the IPM approach. Oil sprays are thin oils that smother insects and coat their eggs to prevent hatching. You can find dormant oils for application during winter, as well as summer oils, which are applied while the tree is in leaf. The fatty acids in horticultural soaps are safe enough to use on edible plants, and they work quickly. But they also lose effectiveness fast. They're best for aphids and other small insects.

⑨ Pesticides are the last step, and sometimes an optional one, in the IPM program. Botanical pesticides such as pyrethrin are made from naturally occurring materials, and are sometimes effective, but do not think that just because these products are "natural" they are nontoxic. Rotenone, for example, is derived from a South American plant, but is death to fish and moderately toxic to mammals.

⑩ Synthetic, or "chemical" pesticides round out the pesticide arsenal. When they first arrived on the scene, following World War II, they were hailed as a

godsend. But as growers and gardeners learned more about chemical pesticides, those apples lost some of their shine. The havoc wrought by DDT encouraged a new generation to take a closer look at what we were spraying on our food. Still, despite continuing concerns about what we spray, captan, benomyl, sulfur and other pesticides are commonly used on fruit trees. If you decide to spray for diseases, you must start at the bud or blossom stage to be effective.

The ideal is to grow kinds and varieties of fruits that will be beset by few or no pest problems and to use trapping, correct siting, pruning and sanitation to keep pests in check. If use of pesticides—either natural or synthetic—becomes necessary, be sure to read and follow all directions with care. Wear long-sleeved pants and shirt and a protective mask over your nose and mouth when using, and wash thoroughly afterward. Never store leftover chemicals in another container, and be sure to dispose of these chemicals correctly, on your local hazardous waste disposal day.

POME FRUITS
Apples & Pears

BY ED FACKLER

APPLES AND PEARS, cultivated since before Christ, are among the most widely planted fruits. And with good reason. If you choose suitable rootstocks and varieties of these pome fruits—fleshy fruits with seeds enclosed in a central papery capsule—you can grow these wonderful treats anywhere in North America. Pome fruit culture can be rewarding in some surprising ways. Dealing with insect and disease pests, for example, can bring its own rewards. Some insect pests are problems only in the larval (worm) stage; as adults, these "pests" become incredibly beautiful butterflies and moths. You might even find the interactions of these pests with your plants interesting, or be fascinated by your tree's responses to pruning. And, of course, there's the delectable fruit.

POME FRUIT ZONES

North America includes three "pome fruit zones." Alaska, Canada and the upper one-fourth of the contiguous states comprise the coldest pome fruit zone. Gardeners in this region should grow varieties that are hardy enough to withstand harsh winter temperatures, and which will mature fruit within the region's relatively short growing season. For recommended varieties see page 30.

The next warmer pome fruit region is bounded to the north by an imaginary line running from Seattle, Washington, to Chicago, Illinois, to Portland, Maine. The southern boundary of this section runs from San Francisco to Tulsa, Oklahoma, to Richmond, Virginia. See page 32 for varieties suited to the region.

How and where you plant your apple or pear tree are crucial factors in its success. Select a site that gets at least six hours of direct sunlight each day during the growing season.

The southern apple and pear region includes everything south of that San Francisco-Tulsa-Richmond line. Apples that do best here must be able to tolerate excessive heat during their ripening stage. For recommendations see page 34.

ROOTS OF GOOD FRUITS

All apple and pear trees are propagated by grafting a scion, which becomes the upper, fruiting part of the tree, onto a rootstock, which will form the roots and lower trunk of the tree. Grafting allows growers to combine the best charac-

Pear trees can take as long as ten years to bear a large crop, but can bear fruit for more than a century, and are generally easier to care for than apple trees.

APPLES & PEARS FOR THE NORTH

VARIETY	RIPENING TIME	COLOR	FLAVOR	COMMENTS
APPLES				
'Norland'	very early	red	good	sweet-tart
'William's Pride'	very early	red	great	disease resistant
'Pristine'	very early	yellow	great	disease resistant
'Redfree'	early	red	good	disease resistant
'State Fair'	early	red	good	very juicy
'Gala'	early-mid	red/yellow	excellent	quick to bear
'Novamac'	mid	red	good	disease resistant
'Honeycrisp'	mid	red	good	disease resistant
'Sweet 16'	mid	red	excellent	large, rosy red fruit
'Fireside'	late	red	good	crisp, large, red
PEARS				
'Summercrisp'	early	red blush	great	fire blight resistant
'Honey Sweet'	mid	red blush	great	fire blight resistant
'Worden Seckel'	mid	red/yellow	great	harvest fully ripe
'Harrow Sweet'	late	yellow	great	fire blight resistant

Asian pears, which are becoming more popular, are usually rounder than European pears, and have flesh that is firm, crunchy, sweet and juicy.

teristics of root and fruit. Both rootstock and scion are chosen for particular characteristics: The scion is propagated by cloning from the tissue of a parent plant to ensure that characteristics of popular varieties such as 'Red Delicious' will not be lost—a possibility when these plants are propagated from seed. Growers select a particular rootstock for its influence on the ultimate size of the tree, or its ability to enhance the tree's drought tolerance, productivity, soil-borne pest resistance and ripening time. The rootstock has little effect on the fruit itself, so a 'MacIntosh' apple will taste and look the same whether it is grown on a very dwarfing rootstock or on a nondwarfing rootstock.

Before you purchase a tree, identify its rootstock. Rootstocks fall into one of three categories: standard, semi-dwarf, and dwarf. Scions grafted onto vigorous or standard rootstock will grow into full-sized, or slightly smaller than full-sized, trees. They are often grafted onto a rootstock named MM111 (after the East Malling Research Station in England where many of the early rootstocks were developed) or onto rootstocks grown from seed. Semi-dwarf rootstocks will produce trees that are 50 to 70 percent of the size of full-sized trees, and most will produce fruit several years earlier. Common semi-dwarf rootstocks include M7, which will produce a tree 50 percent of the size of a standard tree, and MM106, which produces a slightly larger tree. Promising new semi-dwarf rootstocks include Geneva 11, Geneva 16 and Geneva 30. Dwarf rootstocks are excellent for gardeners with limited space. They will produce trees that grow from a maximum height of six feet (M27) to ten feet tall (M26). Trees grafted to the M9 dwarf rootstock will bear fruit within one to two years of planting. Some of the newer, promising, dwarf rootstocks include Bud 9, Geneva 65 and Ottawa 3.

Dwarf pear trees are grown on a variety of quince rootstocks, of which 'Quince C' is the best overall. Good rootstocks for semi-dwarf pears are OHxF 333 and 513. For near standard size pear trees, OHxF 97 and common seedling are used extensively.

POMES FOR THE CENTRAL REGION

VARIETY	RIPENING TIME	COLOR	FLAVOR	COMMENTS
APPLES				
All those listed on page 30 except 'Sweet 16', 'State Fair' and 'Fireside' plus the following:				
'Mollie's Delicious'	early-mid	red	great	very juicy
'Orin'	mid-late	yellow	excellent	
'Jonagold'	mid-late	red	excellent	very juicy, crisp
'Mutsu'	late	yellow/green	excellent	snowy texture
'Shizuka'	late	yellow/green	excellent	
'Fortune'	late	red/maroon	excellent	
'Liberty'	late	red	good	disease resistant
'Spigold'	late	red/green	excellent	very juicy, crisp
'Braeburn'	late	red stripe	excellent	keeps well, juicy
'Enterprise'	late	red	good	disease resistant
'Gold Rush'	late	yellow	great	
'Lady Williams'	very late	red	great	bears quickly
'Pink Lady'	very late	red	good	pink flesh
'Sundowner'	very late	red	great	
PEARS				
'Harrow Delight'	mid	yellow	great	fire blight resistant
'Maxine'	mid	yellow	good	fire blight resistant
'Collette'	mid	yellow	great	fire blight resistant
'Harvest Queen'	late	yellow blush	great	fire blight resistant
'Kosui'	early	green	great	fire blight resistant
'Hosui'	early-mid	brown	great	fire blight resistant
'Niitaka'	mid-late	brown	great	fire blight resistant
'Korean Giant'	mid-late	brown	good	fire blight resistant
'Shin-Li'	late	green	good	fire blight resistant

For tasty, abundant crops, make sure your tree's fruits and leaves—its solar collectors—are not crowded together and hidden from the sun's light.

TRAINING TREES FOR MAXIMUM PRODUCTION

How and where you plant your apple or pear tree are crucial factors in its longevity and productivity. Begin by selecting a site that receives at least six hours of direct sunlight each day during the growing season. Plant in fall or as early in spring as possible. You need to plant at least two trees for cross-pollination, or otherwise provide for pollination, as suggested in "Getting Started," page 11.

Planting depth is critical with most dwarf and semi-dwarf trees. The graft union must be above ground level or else the portion above the rootstock will root, and the dwarfing effect will be lost. Don't set the plant so that the bud union is more than two inches out of the soil, though, because excessive exposure of the root shank can lead to other disorders.

Most dwarf trees have relatively small and brittle root systems and therefore require some sort of support throughout their life. Use a 2" x 2" x 8' stake or other support, a 3- to 4-wire trellis (similar to a grape trellis) or a boundary fence to hold up the plant.

Whatever tree you plant, mulch heavily with some organic material, such as leaves, straw or wood chips. Keep the mulch a couple of inches away from the trunk to discourage rotting and field mouse damage at the base of the trunk. And make sure your tree receives adequate water, especially during its first, critical season in the ground.

THE ART AND SCIENCE OF PRUNING

Train young apple and pear trees as described in "Getting Started," page 11, usually to a central leader form. For semi-dwarf and standard trees, prune as little as is absolutely necessary until the fourth or fifth year, or when they begin to bear fruit. Then select the permanent scaffold limbs and spread or pull them down nearly parallel to the ground. You can do this by tying limbs down with twine or spreading limbs with spreaders made for this purpose. Do this only on a very hot day in late spring or early summer, when wood is relatively flexible.

Most apples bear fruits on short "spurs."

Prune mature apple and pear trees so that they are open to light and air circulation, mainly by removing whole branches rather than simply shortening them. Remember, leaves are, literally, solar collectors, all-important for gathering energy for both tasty and abundant crops, so make sure they get enough light. Apples and pears bear their fruits on short growths called spurs, which, after a few years, become overcrowded. Thin out overcrowded and old spurs to invigorate them and space fruits. Also thin fruits after fruit set. Leave only one fruit, the largest and healthiest one, per cluster.

APPLES & PEARS FOR THE SOUTH

VARIETY	RIPENING TIME	COLOR	FLAVOR	COMMENTS
APPLES				
All those recommended for the Central Region except 'Jonagold' and 'Fortune'				
PEARS				
All those listed on pages 30 and 32 plus the following:				
'Ya-Li'	late	yellow	good	fire blight resistant
'Daisu-Li'	late	brown	good	fire blight resistant

Top: Removing older and overcrowded spurs will invigorate your plant and help you maintain the proper spacing between fruits. Bottom: Thin apples after fruit set, leaving only one fruit, the largest and healthiest, per cluster.

DEALING WITH PESTS

Apples and, to a lesser extent, pears are attacked by several pests that can prevent these trees from producing quality fruit. A simple way to get around at least the disease problem is by planting resistant varieties.

Although apples can be damaged by a host of pests, not all regions have all pests. For example, West Coast gardeners need contend only with codling moth, aphids and, in isolated situations, apple scab. East of the Rockies, major insect pests include plum curculio, codling moth, aphids and, in more northern regions, apple maggot.

Bacterial, fungal and viral diseases that attack pome fruits include apple scab, cedar rust and mildew as well as fire blight, which can wreak havoc with many European pears, causing leaves and stems to look as if they have been blackened by fire. (See pages 30, 32 and 34 for varieties resistant to fire blight.)

Many excellent new apple varieties have been bred for resistance to one or more of the other serious apple diseases. These include 'Pristine', 'William's Pride', 'Redfree', 'Novamac', 'Liberty' and 'Enterprise'. 'Gold Rush' is resistant to

35

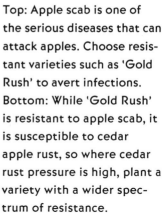

Top: Apple scab is one of the serious diseases that can attack apples. Choose resistant varieties such as 'Gold Rush' to avert infections. Bottom: While 'Gold Rush' is resistant to apple scab, it is susceptible to cedar apple rust, so where cedar rust pressure is high, plant a variety with a wider spectrum of resistance.

scab only and should not be planted where cedar rust pressure is high or if you don't want to use a fungicide for this disease.

A relatively new approach to pest control is to protect fruits with bags made of tinted paper. Place these around individual fruits a few weeks after petal fall. Besides blocking pests, the bags also block sunlight, giving the fruit a paler, more delicate finish. To redden the fruit, remove the bags two weeks before harvest; 'Mutsu', for example, will end up looking like pink porcelain. Bagging also makes the flavor milder.

Control fire blight not only by planting resistant apple varieties, but also by pruning off diseased stems and preventing overly lush growth, which is very susceptible to the disease. Pests other than fire blight can be controlled by a very limited number of pesticide applications (three or four in most seasons) if timing is perfect and trees are pruned to allow maximum air movement and sunlight. Many experimental trials for organic controls of pome fruit pests are underway, but to date, for many pests, researchers have found no organic controls that result in a blemish-free harvest.

Pick apples when their undercolor or ground color changes from a grass green to a softer yellow. You can store your apple harvest in a cool location for many months.

HARVEST AND STORAGE

The most reliable indicator of your fruit's ripeness—other than your own taste buds—is the change in its green undercolor or ground color, from a grass green to a softer yellow green as the fruit ripens. You can also judge your fruit's readiness for harvest by observing changes in seed color. When immature, apple and pear seeds are creamy white, darkening to deep brown as the *Trivia* fruit matures.

Apples and pears can be stored for many months under the right conditions. Both should be stored at temperatures around 30° F (apples can tolerate temperatures up to 40° F) with enough humidity to prevent them from drying out. Cool your fruits to the storage temperature quickly to prevent further ripening. Store them in plastic bags or covered containers with a few holes for air circulation, and add a few drops of water to keep the air inside moist.

STONE FRUITS

Peaches, Plums, Apricots Nectarines & Cherries

BY DAVID CAIN

S INCE THE DAWN OF AGRICULTURE, people have prized and cultivated all the stone fruits for their sweet aromatic flesh and their nutritious protein- and oil-laden kernels, or inner seeds. Over countless plant generations, growers have improved the fruits' qualities by propagating new offspring from the seeds of superior plants. When the great ancient cultures of China and Japan arose there were already many revered varieties; these were disseminated throughout the Old World along the trade routes. Europeans eventually carried cultivated stone fruits to the Americas, where native Americans had already discovered indigenous plum species.

The stone fruits now most widely cultivated include: the peach and its fuzzless mutation the nectarine *(Prunus persica);* apricots *(P. armeniaca* and *P. mandshurica);* European plums (primarily *P. domestica);* Japanese plums (interspecific hybrids involving over five species crossed with *P. salicina);* sweet cherries *(P. avium);* and pie or tart cherries *(P. cerasus).* These species occur naturally over a wide geographic and climatic range, and plant breeders have developed varieties reasonably well adapted to most temperate and subtropical climates.

With careful attention to characteristics such as cold hardiness, winter chilling requirement and resistance to local insects and diseases, you can grow these fruits almost anywhere in the United States. Although any one variety will ripen over a seven- to ten-day period, by carefully choosing varieties that ripen at different times you can have fresh fruit available for three to six months a year, depending on the length of your growing season.

SITE SELECTION

All stone fruit species prefer well-drained sandy loam soils and do poorly in heavy, wet soils. By planting on a mound or ridge rising one to two feet and six to eight feet in diameter, and amending the soil to improve aeration and drainage, you can compensate for the problem posed by heavy soils. Plant trees only as deep as they grew in the nursery. Deeper planting results in weak anchorage and will lead to trunk rot and tree death, especially on heavy soil.

When choosing a planting site, pay careful attention to microclimates. The extra warmth radiated from the south or west side of a building, for example, may help a somewhat tender plant survive winter. A mound of leaves or straw

If your space is limited, you can grow genetic dwarf varieties, like this nectarine, in tubs.

around the trunk during winter adds further protection. On frost-prone sites, cover entire trees with tarps during spring frosts—you may provide enough protection that they will later produce crops. In extreme climates, you can plant trees in large tubs—half whiskey barrels equipped with wheels, for example—and move them into unheated buildings for protection. In subarctic regions of Russia, fruit growers train trees along the ground and bury them each fall to protect them from the bitter winters. The amount of protection you can provide is limited only by your effort and imagination.

✓ Note that most sweet cherries and Japanese plums require cross-pollination; most varieties of peach, nectarine, European plum, tart cherry and apricot are self-fruitful. *Trivia*

VARIETIES

When choosing a variety, consider such fruit qualities as color, size, flavor, ripening time and use (fresh eating, canning, freezing, cooking or pickling). But also consider the plant itself—its size, cold hardiness, disease resistance and time of bloom. Find out the plant's chilling requirement, the number of hours of cold temperatures it requires to resume normal growth in the spring. For most of the United States, high-chill varieties are best. Along the Gulf Coast, Florida and parts of southern Arizona and California, where winters are very warm, plant low-chill varieties, which may need as few as 100 hours of cool temperatures.

If you have limited space you may want to consider genetic dwarf varieties. These varieties grow to five to seven feet tall and are well adapted to pot culture. But since most of them have been bred in California they may lack the hardiness and disease resistance of standard trees.

If you are more adventuresome, you may want to grow more unusual varieties such as white-fleshed peaches and nectarines, green-skinned or red-fleshed plums, yellow cherries, peento peaches or plumcots (hybrids between plums and apricots).

On the following pages, you'll find some commonly available varieties and their characteristics. It's not a comprehensive list—many other fine varieties exist.

ROOTSTOCKS

Rootstocks can impart desirable characteristics to a tree while leaving the fruit itself unaffected. Peaches and nectarines are normally bud-grafted onto peach rootstocks by inserting a single bud of the desired fruiting variety under the bark of the rootstock variety. 'Lovell' peach usually performs best on very sandy soils, although 'Nemaguard' is a better choice where nematodes are a problem. Very hardy rootstocks such as 'Bailey' and 'Siberian C' are best for cold regions like New England. Avoid trees budded onto the dwarfing rootstocks *P.*

RECOMMENDED PEACHES

VARIETY	HARDINESS ZONE	RIPENING TIME	COLOR	FLAVOR	COMMENTS
'Candor'	5-8	early	yellow	good	hardy, disease resistant
'Elegant Lady'	7-8	mid-season	yellow	excellent	not hardy or resistant, firm
'Encore'	5-8	late	yellow	very good	hardy, late blooming
'Flamecrest'	7-8	early	yellow	excellent	not hardy or resistant, firm
'Flordacrest'	9-10	mid-season	yellow	excellent	250 chill hours
'Flordaglo'	9-10	early	white	very good	150 chill hours
'Flordaprince'	9-10	early	yellow	good	150 chill hours
'Garnet Beauty'	5-8	early	yellow	good	Early Redhaven mutation
'Parade'	7-8	very late	yellow	good	moderately hardy & resistant
'Raritan Rose'	6-8	mid-season	white	very good	soft, moderately hardy
'Red Haven'	5-8	mid-season	yellow	excellent	hardy, standard of excellence
'Reliance'	4-6	mid-season	yellow	fair	extremely hardy, blooms late

besseyi and *P. tomentosa,* because these trees are often short-lived. Japanese plums are grafted onto peach rootstocks or onto a plum rootstock such as 'Marianna 2624'. Plum rootstocks generally tolerate cold weather and heavy soils better than do peach rootstocks, and plums such as 'St. Julian C' have also been used as rootstocks for peaches under these conditions. European plums are best

Left: When choosing a variety, think about whether you will eat your harvest fresh, or can, freeze, cook or pickle it.
Below: More than 2,000 varieties of plums are available to the home fruit gardener.

bud-grafted onto 'Brompton' or 'Stanley'. In the West, apricots are normally grown on 'Nemaguard', while apricot seedlings are used in the East.

PRUNING

Most stone fruits are trained to an open-center form, as described in "Getting Started," page 11. Peaches and nectarines flower on wood produced during the previous growing season, while apricots, plums and cherries flower both on the previous season's growth and on spurs, which are short growths that form during the second growing season.

Do most of your pruning while the trees are dormant, preferably just before growth begins in the spring. Remove all large limbs growing into the center of the tree, or arising below the main scaffolds. With peaches and nectarines, retain 12- to 18-inch long, pencil-thick stems spaced evenly around the scaffold limbs. When pruning apricots, plums and cherries, retain limbs that have well-formed spurs, and remove or head back weaker-spurred limbs.

RECOMMENDED NECTARINES & PLUMS

VARIETY	HARDINESS ZONE	RIPENING TIME	COLOR	FLAVOR	COMMENTS
NECTARINES					
'Earliscarlet'	6-8	early	yel	very good	best in mid South
'Harko'	4-7	mid-season	yel	excellent	very hardy, disease resistant
'Redgold'	6-8	mid-season	yel	excellent	hardy, fair disease resistance
EUROPEAN PLUMS					
'Mt. Royal'	4-6	mid-season	blk/yel	very good	very hardy
'Stanley'	5-6	mid-season	blk/yel	good	hardy, self-fertile
JAPANESE PLUMS					
'Gulf Ruby'	9-10	early	red/yel	good	150 chill hours
'Methley'	7-8	early	blk/yel	excellent	adapted to Southeast
'OzarkPremier'	6-8	mid-season	red/yel	very good	adapted to Southeast
'Santa Rosa'	5-8	mid-season	red/yel	excellent	better in arid regions
'Shiro'	5-7	mid-season	grn/yel	very good	hardy, self-infertile
'Superior'	4-8	mid-season	red/yel	very good	very hardy

Apricots bear fruit both on the previous season's growth and on spurs.

In summer, prune back excessively vigorous water sprouts (fast-growing shoots) growing up through the interior of the tree to allow more sunlight to penetrate; this will improve fruit color and quality. Avoid excessive summer pruning, though, especially in hot climates where the scaffold limbs sunburn if they do not receive some shade.

Judge whether or not your tree has been pruned enough by looking at the ground beneath it. You should see at least a few dappled spots of sunlight. If not, prune more.

FRUIT THINNING

Most stone fruit trees bear far more fruit than can properly mature. A crop that is too heavy results in small, low-quality fruit, increased limb breakage, reduced cold hardiness and reduced tree growth, which may result in a smaller crop the following year. Thinning also improves fruit size and sugar content.

Peaches and nectarines require the most thinning. Normally it is more difficult to attain size and quality on early-ripening varieties, so thin them most heavily, to space the fruit ten to twelve inches apart. On mid- and late-season varieties, space fruits six to eight inches apart. Space apricots and plums four to six inches apart on year-old stems, and leave one fruit per spur on older stems. Cherries are rarely thinned commercially, but even they respond to thinning in years when fruit set is especially heavy.

DISEASES AND INSECTS

Stone fruits are susceptible to a wide array of insects and diseases that vary by region. Widespread insect pests include Oriental fruit moth, peach twig borer, plum curculio and scale. Serious and widespread stone-fruit diseases include bacterial spot, peach scab, powdery mildew, cherry leaf spot and brown rot.

RECOMMENDED CHERRIES & APRICOTS

VARIETY	HARDINESS ZONE	RIPENING TIME	COLOR	FLAVOR	COMMENTS
TART CHERRIES					
'Meteor'	4-7	mid-season	red/yel	good	very hardy, self-fertile
'Montmorency'	5-7	mid-season	red/yel	good	old standard, self-fertile
'North Star'	4-8	mid-season	red/yel	good	widely adapted, small tree
SWEET CHERRIES					
'Burlat'	5-8	very early	red	good	needs pollinator
'Hardy Giant'	5-8	mid-season	red	excellent	widely adapted
'Lapins'	5-8	mid-season	red	excellent	self-fertile, better in West
'Rainier'	5-8	mid-season	yel	excellent	cracks, arid regions only
'Van'	5-8	mid-season	red	excellent	very hardy
APRICOTS					
'Goldcot'	4-7	mid-season	yel	fair	cold-hardy
'Hargrand'	4-8	mid-season	yel	excellent	very large
'Patterson'	6-8	late	yel	excellent	arid regions

By learning to tolerate some blemishes on your fruits, you can limit your spraying. But if the problem is severe, you may have to resort to properly timed sprays of organic or conventional chemicals, which must be registered for use on the crop and in the state or locality where they are used and must be applied according to the label recommendations.

Stone fruits are also affected by many serious viral diseases for which there is no cure. Buy certified virus-free trees, control insect vectors and promptly remove and burn infected trees to prevent spread of viral diseases.

HARVEST AND STORAGE

Stone fruits are ready for harvest when the undercolor of the fruit's skin loses its greenish cast and gains its mature color. Pick peaches and nectarines by cradling the fruits gently in your palm and twisting the stems. Ripe fruits will part easily from the tree.

Unlike apples and pears, stone fruits will not last for months on end in storage, but you can keep most for from one to four weeks at 32° F.

STRAWBERRIES

The First Fruit of Spring

BY MARVIN P. PRITTS

THE FAVORITE FRUIT of the goddess Venus, a symbol of the human heart in Cherokee legend, an emblem of the Holy Trinity amongst early Christians and an espoused cure for fever, gout and hypertension: The strawberry is all of these and more. Today, we appreciate the strawberry only for its delectable flavor, but cultures of the past endowed the strawberry with mystical and healing power, and with good reason. Strawberries are an excellent source of vitamin C—even better than oranges—and a good source of fiber. Certain constituents of strawberries are known to be anticarcinogens.

The strawberry—the first fruit of spring—is available in varieties that can grow almost anywhere in the world. Strawberries tolerate a wide range of soil types and are compact yet productive plants that are easy to care for, making them ideal for the home gardener who appreciates the flavor of a strawberry picked at the peak of ripeness.

The origin of the cultivated strawberry *(Fragaria* x *ananassa)* lies in a chance hybridization, in Europe, of *F. virginiana* from eastern North America and *F. chiloensis* from the west coasts of North and South America. From this plant, growers have developed three types of strawberries for cultivation.

Junebearers are the strawberries that, as their name implies, ripen early in the season. Unlike the other two types of strawberries, Junebearers are sensitive

Strawberries can be grown almost anywhere in the world. Because they tolerate a wide range of soil types, are compact yet productive plants and are easy to care for, they are ideal for the home gardener.

to the length of the day, which signals the plant to make above-ground stems called runners (long days) or flowers (short days). "Dayneutral" varieties flower and fruit irrespective of day length, as long as temperatures are not too hot or too cold. The third type of strawberry originated early in the 20th century and was called "everbearer," but bore only two crops each season, an early and a late one. The newer dayneutrals, which might better be called "everbearers," outperform the original everbearers, so the earlier varieties are not worth growing anymore.

SITE PREPARATION

Strawberries grow well in typical garden soils, although a sandy loam with high organic matter and a pH of 6.5 is best. Prevent root rot and other diseases by planting strawberries only in a well-drained soil. Most importantly, the site should be free of perennial weeds, because they are likely to be major pests during the life of the planting. Certain strawberry varieties are susceptible to verticillium wilt disease, which is carried by potatoes, eggplants and members of the rose family. If a strawberry variety is susceptible to verticillium wilt disease, avoid planting it where these plants may have been growing during the last several years.

Top: A netting cover will keep the birds away. Bottom: Mulch strawberries to hold in moisture and keep mud off fruits.

Growing strawberries in colder climates

Junebearers: The most common and least expensive system used to grow strawberries is called the "matted row." Using this method, you encourage strawberry runners to form a dense mat of plants along the row. Obtain dormant plants from a nursery, usually through the mail, in early spring. Plant them about 18 to 24 inches

THE TASTIEST STRAWBERRIES

VARIETY	TYPE/ RIPENING TIME	FREEZING QUALITY	COMMENTS
NORTH, MID-ATLANTIC AND MIDWEST			
'Earliglow'	JB/early	very good	resistant to many diseases; less hardy than other varieties; first variety to ripen
'Jewel'	JB/mid-season	very good	very productive; large, firm fruit
'Sparkle'	JB/late	very good	late to ripen; smaller fruit size; excellent for jam; softer fruit
'Tristar'	DN	good	long fruiting season; resistant to soil diseases; smaller fruit size
NORTHWEST			
'Totem'	JB/late	very good	late maturing; hardy, resistant to red stele virus
'Sumas'	JB	very good	red color throughout; tolerant to viruses; fewer runners
SOUTH			
'Cardinal'	JB/mid-season	good	large, firm fruit; long ripening period; very productive; resistant to leaf diseases
DEEP SOUTH AND CALIFORNIA			
'Chandler'	JB/early	very good	large fruit; long ripening period; susceptible to soil diseases
'Sweet Charlie'	JB	good	somewhat resistant to anthracnose disease; long ripening period

JB=Junebearing; DN=Dayneutral

49

Strawberries will grow well in small spaces and containers, such as this strawberry jar.

apart in single rows, leaving four feet between rows. During the long days of the next several months, runners will produce daughter plants that establish themselves between the original mother plants. Train the runners to form a row no wider than 18 inches to allow ample space to walk between the rows. Remove any flowers on the original mother plant so energy can be devoted to runnering. During this time, plants should be well watered, lightly fertilized and kept weed free. At the end of the first growing season, narrow rows to about 12 to 18 inches wide with a rototiller, leaving at least 2-1/2 feet between matted rows. When the soil has frozen to a depth of one inch in fall or early winter, cover plants with straw mulch to prevent winter injury.

In spring, just as growth commences, uncover the plants, moving the mulch in between the plants to help hold moisture, prevent splashing of mud on the fruit and provide a soft blanket for you to kneel on while picking. Flowers soon appear, followed, about 30 days later, by fruit. A typical variety will fruit for three weeks, and with a selection of early- and late-flowering varieties, you can pick strawberries for up to six weeks. You can place a floating row cover over the bed to accelerate flowering, thereby extending the season. Simply place the row cover over a portion of the bed in early spring, and anchor the edges with bags of sand or shovels of soil. Remove the covers when flowering begins. You can begin your harvest up to two weeks earlier with this method, depending on the weather.

After harvest, mow off the leaves, apply fertilizer and till to narrow the matted row again. This rejuvenates the planting for the following year. After the planting year, these strawberries fruit each spring for several years. The influx of weeds and a decrease in berry size over time will encourage you to start a new planting after about five years.

Dayneutrals: These plants grow best where the summers are cool, as excessively hot temperatures cause the plants to quit flowering. You can harvest your first fruits from these varieties within a few months of planting. Set plants in double rows, rather than in single rows, to increase the number of plants (and yield) in the area. Nine inches between plants is an optimal distance. If the plants in the double rows are staggered (rather than adjacent to each other), yields will be higher. Allow ample room to walk between the double rows, usually about 2-1/2 feet. Mulch dayneutrals with straw after planting, or set them through black plastic to prevent weed growth. Remove any runners that form throughout the season and remove flowers for three to six weeks after planting so that the plant's energy can be used to grow a healthy root system prior to fruiting.

Flowers produced in the seventh week after planting will produce ripe fruit in the eleventh week. While production will be greatest in August and September of the year you plant, you can keep these dayneutrals over the winter, and they will bear fruit in the late spring of the following year. To help them through the winter, mulch them with straw, as described for Junebearers. Dayneutrals have a shorter life span than Junebearers—about two years. Many gardeners treat dayneutral strawberries as annuals, replanting the bed each year.

Since dayneutrals fruit continuously, they require light fertilizer applications at monthly intervals.

Growing strawberries in warmer climates

In climates where strawberry plants do not go dormant during winter, a different growing system is used. Obtain either Junebearing or dayneutral varieties and plant them in August or September. Many row configurations will work but double or triple rows, with plants nine to twelve inches apart, are preferable to single rows. Allow 2-1/2 feet for an alleyway between plant rows. Remove any runners that form, and remove flowers for several weeks to allow plants to establish a strong root system. Plastic can be applied in early spring to warm the soil and accelerate flowering. Since the weather will be cool after planting and the days short, the strawberry plants will stay in a flowering mode for several months. Lightly fertilize plants at regular intervals. In summer the plants may stop fruiting because of the heat. Replant each year to ensure good yields.

The most troublesome strawberry disease is gray mold, which infects flower parts during rainy weather. Renovating beds, mulching and picking off infected fruits will help ward off this fungus.

Strawberries become "cat faced" or seedy when they are fed upon by the most common strawberry pest, the plant bug; dayneutral strawberries are especially susceptible to this pest.

STRAWBERRY PESTS

Strawberries' most common insect pest is the plant bug, which causes fruits to be "catfaced," or seedy, at their ends; dayneutral varieties are very susceptible to this insect. Mites, aphids and sap beetles commonly feed on the above-ground portions of strawberry plants, while weevil larvae and grubs feed on plant roots. These pests may be found wherever strawberries are grown.

Strawberries are also susceptible to certain bacterial, fungal and viral diseases, especially during rainy weather. The most troublesome is gray mold, a fungus that attacks strawberry fruits. During wet weather, the fungus infects the flower parts and produces spores on the berries when they ripen. Other fruit diseases include leather rot, which causes a bitter taste, and anthracnose, which leaves black spots on the fruit. In warm climates, anthracnose disease causes the plants to collapse as if they were not receiving sufficient water, and several root-rotting fungi cause similar symptoms. Good soil drainage and weed-free fields create an environment unfavorable for many insect and disease organisms, so plant on raised beds in all but the sandiest soils, and do not allow weeds to become established.

Strawberries not only have a delectable flavor but are high in vitamin C and fiber.

HARVEST AND STORAGE

The major advantage of growing your own strawberries is the flavor of freshly harvested berries, which is incomparably better than that of strawberries shipped from distant fields. To enjoy their full flavor and sweetness, strawberries should not be harvested until they are completely red. Although strawberries will turn red after harvest, they will not increase in sweetness or flavor. If strawberries must be stored for several days, cool them to about 32° F as soon as possible after harvest, then wrap them in plastic wrap to prevent moisture loss. Any delay in cooling will shorten their storage life significantly. Strawberries can be frozen for use at a later date; temperatures near 0° F are recommended. Some varieties are better for freezing than others.

53

Flowers, Fruits & Fiery Foliage

BY DANIEL HARTMANN

AMONG PLANTS THAT BEAR FRUIT and have year-round beauty, the blueberry is a standout. The stems are clothed in dainty white, bell-shaped flowers in spring, then soft green foliage throughout summer; by fall, the foliage is fiery crimson; and in winter, reddish stems await spring's return. Blueberries can be grown almost anywhere in the United States, and with proper encouragement, will thrive in your garden.

PREPARING YOUR SITE

One of the most important factors in blueberry cultivation is to provide the proper soil conditions, which means acidity, good drainage and abundant organic matter. If the soil pH is higher that 4.5 to 5.5, mix in sulfur at least four weeks before planting. Add from about a half to five pounds, depending on the initial pH and the soil texture: sandier soils require less sulfur than heavier soils. Dig a planting hole 18 inches deep and at least 12 inches in diameter, and mix equal parts Canadian peat moss and soil to provide organic matter.

Blueberry plants are available bare-root or potted. Before planting a potted blueberry, tease the roots away from the outside of the rootball to help coax

Blueberries are a garden standout in the spring (below), when they are covered with dainty bell-shaped flowers; in the summer (above) when they are covered with luscious fruits; and in the fall and winter, when foliage then stems turn fiery red.

them to grow out into the surrounding soil. Otherwise, even after planting, the roots may continue to grow in a circular motion for a year or more as if they were still growing in the container. Keep the roots of bare-root plants wet by soaking them in a bucket of water for six hours when you receive the bushes, then keep them moist with a covering of damp burlap, sawdust or leaves until you actually set the plants in the ground.

Planting depth is critical. The crown of the plant—where the roots begin along the stem—should be no deeper than 1/4 to 1/2 inch beneath ground level. After planting, spread an organic mulch around the planted area to a depth of four inches.

With proper encouragement—the right soil conditions, proper planting depth and good pruning—blueberries will thrive in your garden.

A few species grown in the United States have been extensively hybridized to create fruits with a range of characteristics, such as cold-hardiness, ripening season, disease resistance, berry size and flavor. These five are northern and southern highbush *(Vaccinium corymbosum* and hybrids), half-high (hybrids of highbush and lowbush), rabbiteye *(V. ashei)*, and lowbush (mostly *V. angustifolium* and *V. myrtilloides)*. (Varieties of lowbush blueberries exist, but, for the most part, growers cultivate bushes from seedlings or wild plants, so lowbush blueberries are not included in the lists on pages 57 and 59. Lowbush blueberries spread by underground stems to blanket an area, and range in height from 10 to 24 inches.)

Blueberries do not absolutely require cross-pollination, but planting two different varieties near each other does increase yield and berry size.

THE BEST BLUEBERRIES

VARIETY	ZONE	RIPENING TIME	FLAVOR	HEIGHT	YIELD IN LBS
HIGHBUSH					
'Berkeley'	5-7	mid-season	mild/good	5'-6'	5
'Blue Crop'	4-7	mid-season	good	4'-6'	10-20
'Blue Gold'	4-7	early-mid	good	4'-5'	10-15
'Blue Jay'	4-7	early-mid	fair	5'-7'	10-15
'Blue Ray'	4-7	early-mid	excellent	5'-7'	10-20
'Bluetta'	5-7	early	good	3'-5'	10-15
'Collins'	5-7	early-mid	excellent	4'-6'	10-15
'Coville'	5-7	mid-late	excellent	4'-6'	5-8
'Duke'	4-7	early	good	4'-6'	10-20
'Earliblue'	4-7	early	good	4'-6'	5-10
'Elliott'	4-7	late	acid/fair	4'-6'	10-20
'Jersey'	4-7	late	excellent	5'-7'	10-15
'Nelson'	4-7	late-mid	excellent	5'-7'	10-20
'Northland'	3-7	early-mid	excellent	3'-4'	10-20
'Patriot'	3-7	early-mid	good	4'-6'	10-20
'Sierra'	4-7	early-mid	excellent	4'-6'	10-20
'Spartan'	5-7	early-mid	excellent	5'-7'	10-20
'Toro'	4-7	mid	excellent	5'-7'	10-20

PRUNING

Many blueberry growers attribute their success to proper pruning, which they do during the dormant season while the plants are leafless. During the first three years that your blueberries are in the ground, prune off 80 to 100 percent of the fruit buds to encourage new growth for good production in future years. Fruit buds are the fatter buds that form toward the ends of year-old stems. Also remove any horizontal or drooping branches, to direct energy into upright growth.

When your plants reach their fourth year and thereafter, begin to thin out older stems, which become less productive. Cut any stems that are five or more years old down to the ground or to low, vigorous side branches. Young, fruitful stems originating from or near ground level will replace those old stems. Also cut back any low or drooping stems, so the bush remains upright, and cut away twiggy growth in the center of the bush and around the base of the plant.

Before pruning, established blueberries may have many older, less productive stems (left). Cut stems five years or older to the ground or to low, vigorous side branches, and cut back any low or drooping stems. The pruned bush (right) should be upright and no longer have any twiggy growth at its center.

Lowbush blueberries are easier to prune. Every three to four years, or when you notice that the plants are no longer dense with leaves, cut all growth back to one to two inches. You can do this with hand pruners, hedger shears or a lawn mower if plants are well established.

To ensure yourself of fruit every year, divide your established lowbush blueberry bed into halves, thirds or quarters, and prune a different half, third or quarter every two, three or four years. You will not harvest a crop from those plants that have undergone dormant pruning the previous season, but you will from all the others.

THE BEST BLUEBERRIES

VARIETY	ZONE	RIPENING TIME	FLAVOR	HEIGHT	YIELD IN LBS
RABBITEYE					
'Bonita Blue'	8-9	early	excellent	5'-10'	8-12
'Brightwell'	7-9	late-mid	good	8'-12'	8-14
'Climax'	7-9	mid	good	6'-10'	8-20
'Powderblue'	7-9	late	good	5'-8'	8-14
'Premier'	7-9	mid	excellent	5'-8'	8-16
'Tifblue'	7-9	late	good	8'-14'	8-25
HALF-HIGH					
'Friendship'	3-7	mid	good	3'-4'	4-8
'North Country'	3-7	early-mid	fair	18"-24"	2-7
'Northblue'	3-7	early	fair	18"-24"	2-7
'Northsky'	3-7	early-mid	good	18"	2-7
'St. Cloud'	3-7	early	good	24"-30"	4-8
SOUTHERN HIGHBUSH					
'Georgia Gem'	7-9	early-mid	good	5'-6'	8-15
'Misty'	6-10	early	excellent	6'	8-15
'O'Neal'	7-9	early-mid	good	6'	8-15
'Reveille'	7-8	early-mid	good	6'	8-15
'Sharpblue'	7-10	early	excellent	6'	8-15

DETERRING BIRDS

Birds love blueberries, and may strip the fruit clean from unprotected bushes. You can most effectively protect your bushes with netting. Support the net above the plants with a wood or plastic framework, and anchor the net to the ground. Birds will fly right beneath netting that is just draped over bushes.

There are alternatives to netting—a variety of scare devices—but they don't work as well. "Predator bird scare" balloons have designs similar to a large hawk's eyes, and are most effective if moved periodically and used against flocking birds. Another deterrent is flashy mylar tape, about 1/2-inch wide with bright silver on one side and red on the other, draped around the bush.

Top: Lowbush blueberries, which are mainly cultivated from seedlings or wild plants, will quickly spread by underground stems to blanket an area.

Bottom: Your blueberries will not achieve maximum flavor until a few days after the berries turn blue—then your patience will pay off.

PESTS AND DISEASES

Fungal diseases are minimal on blueberries, but include anthracnose, alternaria, cane cankers, botrytis and mummyberry. To limit these diseases, avoid over-fertilizing and prune out diseased stems. By thoroughly cleaning up berries at the end of the season and using a thick, organic mulch, you should be able to control mummyberry. If these methods fail, you may have to turn to sprays.

Insects are not an important threat to blueberries, but the bushes are sometimes attacked by aphids, blueberry maggot, cranberry fruitworm and Japanese beetles. Try handpicking, water or soap sprays, or traps (red sticky spheres for blueberry maggot) before resorting to sprays.

"Predator bird scare" balloons appear to have large hawk's eyes, and are most effective against flocking birds.

ENJOYING YOUR HARVEST

With harvest time comes your reward. Don't harvest blueberries as soon as the fruits turn blue: They need another few days to develop full flavor. Pick blueberries by tickling the fruit clusters with your fingers, so that only the ripe ones drop off into your hand.

You can harvest lowbush blueberries in quantity (at some sacrifice of fresh, but not cooked, flavor) by using a blueberry rake, which resembles a dustpan with tines. As the stems run through the tines, the berries pop off into the "dustpan." You do have to take the time to separate leaves and green berries from the ripe berries. The leaves need not be wasted, though—they make a delicious, healthy tea.

Raspberries & Blackberries

BY PAUL M. OTTEN

BRAMBLE FRUITS ARE AS near to a perfect fruit as you'll find. They've got eye appeal and exquisite flavor and are rich in nutrients and fiber, yet low in calories. Brambles can be grown almost anywhere the climate is not extreme, the soil is reasonably good and water and sunlight are available.

Bramble berries come in a variety of colors and flavors. Mention raspberries, and people think red. But they can also be black, purple and yellow. Purple raspberries are the result of crosses between blacks and reds, while yellow raspberries are mutations of red ones. Blackberries are only available in one color: black. You can differentiate a black raspberry from a blackberry by picking the fruit: raspberries leave the receptacle on the plant, so are hollow like a thimble; blackberries retain the receptacle with the picked fruit. All cultivated brambles are self-fruitful.

Brambles have perennial roots, but the stems, or "canes," are biennial, dying back by their second winter. "Summerbearers" produce their berries on canes that grew the previous season. "Fallbearers" produce their crop on canes of the current growing season, and are easier to grow than summerbearers. Blackberries are available only as summerbearers, but some can bear into early fall.

Blackberries, like all bramble fruits, have eye appeal and exquisite flavor, and are rich in nutrients and fiber, yet low in calories. Brambles can be grown almost anywhere the climate is not extreme, the soil is reasonably good and there's abundant sunshine and rain.

CHOOSING THE RIGHT SPOT

Selecting a good site for brambles is important. For the best tasting berries and most productive plants, choose a spot with full sun protected from open winds. Red raspberries are the most cold hardy of the group and do better in cooler regions. Blackberries, erect, semi-erect and trailing in habit, are less winter hardy than black or purple raspberries and thrive in warmer regions. Generally, the erect varieties are most winter hardy, the trailing least. ('Illini Hardy' is most cold hardy, followed by 'Chester', 'Darrow', 'Shawnee' and 'Cherokee'.)

Berry plants grow best in a well-drained soil with an organic content of 3 percent or more. Add large quantities of organic matter—preferably high quality compost—frequently. All brambles thrive in the cool, moist soil beneath an organic mulch such as leaves, wood chips or straw, replenished annually or as needed. Mulch also suppresses weeds and further enriches the soil with organic matter. Throughout the growing season, plants should receive the equivalent of one to two inches of water each week.

THE BEST RASPBERRIES

	HARDINESS ZONE	TYPE/COLOR	FLAVOR	COMMENTS
'Algonquin'	4b	SB/red	very good	RR, MV, SB, BD
'Allen'	4b	SB/black	good	concentrated harvest
'Amity'	4b	FB/red	good	RR, SB
'Autumn Bliss'	3a	FB/red	very good	very early season; RR, MV
'Bababerry'	6a	S&FB/red	good	most heat tolerant
'Blackhawk'	4b	SB/black	good	large fruits; BD
'Boyne'	3a	SB/dark red	good	early season; RR, BD
'Brandywine'	4b	SB/purple	good	very late ripening
'Bristol'	5a	SB/black	very good	very large fruits; PM, BD
'Canby'	5a	SB/light red	excellent	superior flavor, no spines
'Chilliwack'	5b	SB/red	excellent	X-large fruit; RR, MV, SB, BD
'Estate'	4b	SB/purple	good	very late ripening; PM
'Haut'	5a	SB/black	very good	late ripening; medium size
'Heritage'	5a	FB/red	good	upright canes; RR
'Jewel'	4b	SB/black	very good	least susceptible of blacks
'Killarney'	3b	SB/red	good	large fruits; RR, MV, BD
'Munger'	5a	SB/black	excellent	early ripening; medium size
'Nordic'	3a	S&FB/red	good	tolerates heat well; RR, MV
'Nova'	4a	SB/light red	good	good yield and quality
'Redwing'	3a	FB/red	very good	very early season
'Royalty'*	4b	SB/purple	very good	extra large fruit; RR, MV
'Willamette'	6b	SB/red	good	tolerates heat; CG, PM, BD

FB=fallbearing, SB=summerbearing

The following denote diseases to which plants are resistant: CG=crown gall; RR=root rot; MV=mosaic virus; PM=powdery mildew; SB=spur blight; BD=bushy dwarf.

VARIETIES

Not only do bramble varieties show differences in fruit characteristics such as berry flavor, size and ripening season, but they also vary in plant hardiness and resistance to various pests. Take these differences, which are detailed in nursery

Scottish fruit researchers crossed the blackberry 'Aurora' and a red raspberry, and the tayberry was born. Grow tayberries as you would blackberries: They have similar growth characteristics and climatic requirements. The plants are moderately vigorous and prickly.

catalogs, into account when choosing which varieties to plant. If you want a continuous supply of bramble fruit, plant both summerbearing and fallbearing brambles with a variety of maturity dates.

If you live in a northern region, make sure you get summerbearing brambles with canes that are sufficiently cold hardy for your area. Because root systems of brambles are rarely damaged by cold, there's no need to worry about winter damage to fallbearing raspberries; you will prune the canes down to the ground each year anyway. With fallbearers, the chief question is: Do they ripen early enough to escape the first severe fall frosts?

The farther south you live, the greater attention you should pay to a variety's minimum chill hours and heat tolerance. In the extreme South, select a site where plants will be partially or fully shaded from noon to four o'clock. Shade

THE BEST BLACKBERRIES

	HARDINESS ZONE	FLAVOR	COMMENTS
'Arapaho'	6a	superior	earliest of blacks
'Brazos'	7b	good/tart	disease-resistant, leading southern cultivar
'Cherokee'	5a	good	sweet, second most hardy
'Chester'	5a	very good	very long season, hardy; large, sweet fruits
'Hull'	5b	sweet	very large fruits, fairly hardy
'Illini Hardy'	4b	fair-good	very winter hardy
'Navaho'	5b	excellent	very late, very disease resistant

cloth material, which filters out much of the sun's rays, can minimize heat stress.

PLANTING

Red and yellow bramble varieties multiply by sending up new shoots either from the crown or from lateral buds on spreading roots. Black and purple raspberries develop new plants by tip-layering: When the tip of a long stem arches over and touches the ground, it takes root. (The variety 'Royalty' is an exception.) Blackberries generally multiply as new shoots arise from their roots.

Plant dormant brambles in very early spring. Set them so that the root

Blackberries are available only as summerbearers, but some will continue to bear their sweet fruits into early fall.

Prune blackberries by removing the canes that have fruited immediately after harvest. In early spring, cut away all but the sturdiest five or six canes in each clump, and cut lateral branches back to 12-18 inches. Before (right) and after (left) pruning.

mass is spread out and covered with two to three inches of soil. Firm the soil well and keep it moist for the first few months. Cut back any top growth on dormant plants right after you set them in the ground.

Fallbearing raspberries spread 12 to 15 inches per year in all directions, so plant them about a foot apart if you want a full row by fall, farther apart if you are willing to wait longer. Summerbearing raspberries may be set from one to three feet apart. Set blackberries and black and purple raspberries three or more feet apart, depending on the vigor of the variety.

To limit spread of these plants beyond the planting area, place wooden or plastic barriers in the ground. Dig down about 10 to 12 inches and place the boards or plastic barrier at the desired border. Allow the base of the planted row to spread 12 to 18 inches across. If you do not use barriers, hoe or till very shallowly or, even better, mow plant tops regularly when they extend out of bounds.

Trellising—attaching plants to one or more wires strung between posts sunk into the ground—is not essential for fallbearers, but does keep their canes upright. Other types of brambles benefit considerably from trellising, which also makes harvesting easier.

PRUNING

When it comes to pruning, divide brambles into three groups: all fallbearing raspberries; summerbearing red and yellow raspberries; and black raspberries, purple raspberries and blackberries.

Fallbearing raspberries are the easiest to prune. At the end of the winter, when the snow is gone, just mow or cut all the canes down to the ground. If you have a wood chipper, grind them up, compost them, and return the resulting organic matter back to the field next year.

Individual canes of summerbearing red and yellow raspberries grow up one year, overwinter, produce a crop the second summer, then die. Because they die, they must be removed to allow for space, air circulation and sunlight. On a dry day immediately after the harvest, cut these spent canes to the ground, then carefully remove them without damaging the softer new canes. You will have too many young canes, so thin them out: Leave the sturdiest ones, no closer than six inches apart, and cut the extra ones to the ground. During the dormant season either shorten your remaining sturdy canes or weave them into the wire(s), depending on the height of your trellis and the length of the canes, so that they do not flop around in the wind.

Blackberries and black and purple raspberries grow in clumps if the tips of stems are not allowed to touch the ground and take root. As with the summerbearing raspberries, right after harvest remove canes that have fruited; they will die anyway. As new growth begins in spring, allow only the heaviest five or six canes to grow up in each clump, and remove the rest. When the new canes are about waist high, cut off the top three to six inches to force growth of lateral branches, which will bear the fruit the following year. Even these lateral branches have to be thinned. In late winter or very early spring, remove all but the largest eight to ten branches per cane, and then cut them back to no more than 8 to 12 inches in length. Fewer canes, and fewer and shorter branches, reduce the number of berries but increase the size of those that remain and promote the plants' health by letting them bathe in sun and air.

All brambles should be picked early in the morning, when fully ripe—they'll separate easily from the plant. Wash or rinse them just before eating or processing.

DISEASES AND PESTS

Brambles suffer mainly from fungal infestations, including anthracnose, spur blight and cane blight. Severe infestations require spraying with liquid lime-sulfur, a natural but smelly product, to cover all canes just as the first leaves begin to emerge in early spring. Limit summerbearing brambles to two or three bearing canes per square foot so that they are exposed to enough air and sunlight to inhibit the growth of these fungi.

Insects, such as Japanese beetles in the eastern states, are occasional problems, but usually are little cause for concern for home gardeners. If you encounter insect or disease problems, consult your county extension specialist.

HARVESTING AND STORING

Don't pick brambles until they are fully ripe, at which time they separate easily from the plant. Pick into very shallow containers early in the morning, when the berries are coolest but after the dew is off. Keep berries as close as possible to freezing temperatures, and their shelf life will be longer and flavor better. Wash or rinse them just before using, serving or processing. For winter use, try freezing whole berries on a cookie sheet, bagging them only after they are fully frozen. If you have a dehydrator, look for simple fruit leather recipes to make delicious blended sheets of berries.

GRAPES
The Versatile Vine

BY LON J. ROMBOUGH

GRAPES ARE AMONG THE widest ranging and most adaptable of fruits, and can be grown from the tropics to Siberia. They are also among the fruits with the most diverse uses: Grapes can be turned into juice, jelly, wine, raisins or simply eaten fresh. The grape varieties available from nurseries fall into four groups.

American hybrid grapes such as 'Buffalo' are crosses between native fox grapes, other American varieties and *vinifera,* or European, wine grapes.

'Concord' grapes are hardy and disease-resistant, with highly flavored berries.

American hybrid 'Kay Gray', a small-clustered sweet grape, tolerates cold well.

The *vinifera,* or European wine grape *(Vitis vinifera),* is the oldest cultivated species, having arisen in the Middle East where wild forms still exist. This grape was first selected for wine and drying, then later (though still within Biblical times) for table fruit. *Vinifera* is the main grape of commerce, and its appealing qualities include high sugar content, which keeps dried grapes from spoiling and yields enough alcohol during fermentation to preserve wine; mild, sometimes fresh "muscat" or flowery, aromatic flavor, plus distinctive flavors in wine; firm, meaty flesh; tender skin; and seedlessness, if desired.

Vinifera grapes grow easily from cuttings and are generally vigorous, productive and manageable. These grapes tolerate alkaline soils and desert heat, but have little tolerance for winter cold or American grape pests. Most *vinifera* grapes are hardy to about -5° F, while a few northern European varieties tolerate winter lows down to -20° F. *Vinifera* grapes grow best where winters are mild and summers have low humidity and little rain, so do poorly in much of the United States outside the West and Southwest unless sprayed heavily, protected in winter and grafted to special rootstocks.

In America, colonists turned to native grapes for disease resistance and hardiness. Their main choice was the fox grape *(V. labrusca),* which bears large,

Grape vines look magnificent almost anywhere they are grown.

Vinifera grapes, the oldest cultivated species, are vigorous and productive.

attractive berries with the strong flavor typified in the well-known 'Concord' variety. The fox grape is the main species of the so-called *American hybrid* varieties, most of which also contain genes of other American species and even *vinifera* types.

The introduction of American grape pests to France in the middle 1800s decimated vineyards there and stimulated development of new, pest-resistant varieties. Breeders such as Seibel, Baco, Seyve-Villard and others crossed vinifera with American species to get so-called *French hybrid* grapes. The fruits of French hybrids resemble viniferas more than American hybrids, and most are grown for wine, although a few are good table grapes. They vary in both cold-hardiness and pest resistance. Most bear the breeder's name and a number, e.g. Seibel 1000, rather than variety names.

In the southeastern United States, yet another grape has attained prominence: the *muscadine* grape *(V. rotundifolia),* a native species that can tolerate the pests fostered in this hot, humid climate. In contrast to other types of grapes—collectively called "bunch grapes" because they hold onto their many berries in a bunch—muscadines have small clusters of three to five berries, and the individual berries drop as they ripen. Individual berries can be large, over an inch in diameter, and dull purple, black, green or bronze. They have an intense aroma and taste somewhat like a refined, perfumed fox grape. The best way to harvest them is to shake the vines over a sheet spread on the ground. Muscadines require the longest season of all grapes, and they bloom and set fruit on the new growth until early to mid-summer. Over the past 90 years, breeders have created varieties with more tender skins than those found on wild types and older varieties, and that bear seedless berries.

Except for some varieties of muscadines that need separate pollinator plants, all cultivated grapes are self-fruitful.

VARIETY	TYPE	COMMENTS
NORTHEAST		
'Bluebell'	AH	blue, seeded, for dessert and juice
'Buffalo'	AH	blue, seeded, for dessert and juice
'Campbell Early'	AH	blue, seeded, for dessert and juice
'Edelweiss'	AH	white, seeded, for dessert and juice
'Kay Gray'	AH	white, seeded, for dessert and juice
'N.Y. Muscat'	AH	red-blue, seeded, for dessert and wine
'Swenson Red'	AH	red, seeded, for dessert and wine
LOWER MIDWEST		
'Albania'	AH	white, seeded, for dessert, wine and juice
'Beacon'	AH	black, seeded for dessert and juice
'Manito'	AH	black, seeded, for dessert
'Valhalla'	AH	red, seeded, for dessert, wine and juice
'Villard Blanc'	FH	white, seeded, for dessert and wine
DEEP SOUTH		
'Carlos'	M	bronze, seeded, for juice and wine
'Golden Isles'	M	bronze, seeded, for wine and juice
'Triumph'	M	pink-bronze, seeded, for dessert and juice
LOWER WEST		
'Beauty Seedless'	V	black, seedless, for dessert
'Early Muscat'	V	white, seeded, for dessert and wine
'Flame'	V	red, seedless, for dessert and raisins
'Malaga'	V	red, seeded, for dessert
'Ribier'	V	black, seeded, for dessert
'Thompson Seedless'	V	white, seedless, for dessert, raisins and wine
PACIFIC NORTHWEST		
'Aurore'	FH	white, seeded, for dessert, wine and juice
'Einset'	AH	red, seedless, for dessert
'Interlaken'	AH	white, seeded, for dessert and raisins
'Marechal Foch'	FH	black, seeded, for wine and juice
'Reliance'	AH	red, seedless, for dessert and juice
'Vanessa'	AH	pale red, seedless, for dessert

AH=American hybrid; FH=French hybrid; V=*vinifera;* M=muscadine

Before pruning, grapes grown using the cordon system will have numerous leggy canes sprouting from these permanent arms.

VARIETIES

Worldwide, there are an estimated 10,000 to 20,000 grape varieties, with at least 2,000 to 5,000 American varieties. The chart on page 75 lists a number of varieties that have proven easy to grow in the regions specified. Varieties suggested for one region may also do well in other regions, and, aside from the varieties listed, there are others that may do well, or at least succeed, but only with careful spraying and protection from adverse climatic conditions. In other words, the listed varieties are not the only ones worth trying.

PRUNING AND TRAINING

Grapes fruit on shoots arising from one-year-old stems, called canes. Prune during the dormant season, removing 85 to 95 percent of the previous summer's

Cut all canes along the cordons to two- to four-bud spurs. On young vines, leave no more than 12 spurs.

growth, in order to regulate crop load and to keep the vine to a manageable size and form. Grapes have been trained to many systems, most variations of two basic methods: cane pruning or spur pruning.

In *cane pruning,* the vine is trained so that it has a single, permanent trunk off which grow long canes. Each year shorten canes to ten to 15 buds each. Depending on variety, vigor and vine age, you might leave four to six canes, or a total of 45 to 90 fruit buds. To ensure a supply of shoots originating near the trunk, which will become next season's fruiting canes, also leave some short stems, called spurs, along the trunk, each one or two buds long and originating near an existing cane.

After pruning, tie the fruiting canes to horizontal support wires. Two or more wires may be used, each at least a foot apart. Either tie canes along wires, or bring canes up to an upper wire, then bend them down in an arch, tying them also to a lower wire. Or train them in a fan shape starting near ground level. The fan system is often used where sunlight is restricted.

77

Phylloxera, the most serious grape pest, feeds on roots of susceptible vines. In the eastern United States, a flying form makes galls like these on grape leaves.

In *spur pruning,* all canes are cut to two- to four-bud spurs that arise directly from the trunk of the vine, or are distributed along permanent arms—called "cordons"—that branch off the trunk. This arrangement is good for table grapes because it distributes the fruit evenly and makes disease control easier. On young vines, leave no more than twelve spurs.

If a vine bears too many fruits, they may ripen late, with poor color and flavor. Overcropping also weakens the vine, making it more vulnerable to winter injury and reducing the following year's crop. Experience will allow you to gauge how large a crop can be ripened, and then you can adjust it by pruning more severely or by clipping off some flower clusters at bloom time.

Many American varieties can be either spur or cane pruned, although some— 'Canadice', 'Schuyler' and 'Alden', for example—are so productive that they need spur pruning to only two-bud spurs and then crop thinning to prevent overload. Varieties such as 'Himrod', 'Seneca' and 'Vanessa' must be cane pruned because their lower buds are unproductive. Grapes with small clusters (many wine grapes) should be pruned to canes long enough to leave plenty of buds, hence plenty of fruit clusters and pounds of fruit per vine. Train muscadines to spurs on long cordons, six to nine feet, because these vigorous growers can support heavy crops.

In cold climates, train vines to two or even three trunks, rather than one. Multiple trunks increase the chances that at least one trunk will survive a frigid winter. Because multiple trunks are individually thinner and more flexible than a single trunk, you also could bend down a cold-tender variety and protect it in winter beneath a covering of soil or mulch.

Black rot, a fungal disease, shrivels and mummifies berries and kills leaves.

DISEASES AND PESTS

Where summers are warm and there is regular rainfall and/or high humidity, four fungal diseases attack susceptible grape varieties: downy mildew, powdery mildew, black rot and anthracnose, or bird's eye rot. Downy mildew forms a "furry" gray fungal mass on the leaves and fruit. Powdery mildew shows up as a white or gray dusting on the leaves and a gray dust or net on the fruit, and is one disease that thrives where summers are hot and dry. Black rot causes shriveling and mummification of berries as well as the death of leaves. Anthracnose on leaves causes black spots with yellow borders; on fruits, it results in black, sunken spots. Disease intensity varies with environmental conditions and susceptibility of the variety. Few modern varieties resist all four diseases completely, although some older types are very resistant.

In the Southeast, Pierce's Disease is a serious bacterial disease that weakens or kills affected vines. There is no cure—vines must be resistant. Muscadines are the main resistant grapes, although bunch grapes have been bred with resistance. Other bacterial diseases affecting the vine include crown gall, which appears as a warty growth at the base of the trunk and crops up on plants suffering from mechanical damage or sunburn, and dead-arm, a disease that causes the fruiting arms of the plant to die off. But these only appear sporadically and are not often lethal. Replace vines infected with crown gall, and prune off parts attacked by dead-arm.

The most serious insect of grapes is phylloxera, which feeds on roots of susceptible vines, usually *vinifera* grapes, stunting and deforming them, and seriously weakening the vines. In the East, a flying form makes galls on the leaves. Vines in infested soil must either be able to resist the pests or be grafted to resistant rootstocks. Most American varieties tolerate mild infestations.

'Muscat' grapes have a distinctive flavor—fresh, flowery and aromatic.

'Flame' grapes are seedless, and perfect for dessert and for making raisins.

HARVEST AND STORAGE

Blue, black and red table grapes are usually edible when they color, but a few, such as 'Campbell's Early', should be left on the vine a little longer to develop more sweetness. Green or yellow grapes become translucent when ripe and lose their grass-green color. But your taste buds will be your best guide to ripeness. Don't be hasty to harvest—grapes stop ripening, and sweetening, when harvested. If you are growing grapes for wine, you will have to measure the sugar content of the grapes before harvesting, using a refractometer or hydrometer, to be certain there is enough sugar to make wine.

If you are going to store your grapes, groom clusters by clipping spoiled or damaged berries off at the stem using scissors or needle-nosed florist shears. Do not pull these berries off, because you will leave a wet "brush" that can serve as the entry point for rot. Lay grape clusters in shallow layers no more than two to three clusters deep in a clean wooden or wicker container. Grapes will spoil faster in plastic or other non-breathing containers. At 32° F, you can store grapes for as long as six months. Some of the grapes will shrivel, but will still taste good.

OFFBEAT & UNUSUAL FRUITS
Branching Out

BY LEE REICH

READY TO BRANCH OUT beyond apples, peaches, plums and strawberries? You may want to plant some of the following rarely grown fruits for their uncommonly delicious flavors and because they are so easy to grow; these rare birds can take frigid winters and require little or no pruning or spraying. You also may want to plant these fruits for the beauty of the plants themselves; some uncommon fruits are not uncommon—as ornamentals. And you may want to plant some of these fruits because that's the only way

You may want to plant some offbeat fruits—like gooseberries and black and red currants (seen below with raspberries)—because that's the only way you'll get to eat them.

Pawpaw, a North American native, bears a fruit the size and shape of a mango. It tastes like banana with hints of mango, pineapple and avocado.

you'll get to eat them. After all, if you have ever tasted and enjoyed a pawpaw, how are you going to assure yourself of a regular supply of this rare fruit except by growing it?

PAWPAW

Pawpaw *(Asimina triloba,* Zones 5 to 8) is a good place to begin this sampling of uncommon fruits. Here is a native of eastern North America that can tolerate winter temperatures that plummet to below -25° F, yet bears a fruit that has the taste and texture of banana with flavor hints of mango, pineapple and avocado. Sometimes called the Michigan or Hoosier banana, pawpaw fruits are the size and shape of a mango, with skin that turns from green to yellow, speckled with brown, as it ripens in late summer and fall.

The whole tree, in fact, has a tropical air to it. The leaves are large and lush like those of avocado, and the flowers are lurid purple. The flowers need cross-pollination, and no one is quite sure just what insect does this job. Suitable pollinators, whatever they are, are sometimes absent. If pollination is a problem, just hand pollinate, transferring the pollen from one plant to the next with a small

Juneberries grow wild throughout the United States and have sweet and juicy fruit, with the richness of sweet cherry and a hint of almond flavor.

paintbrush. This is a rewarding job because each flower is a multiple ovary that can give rise to a cluster of fruits (just like a bunch of bananas). Your yield then becomes limited only by how much fruit the branches can support. Occasional pruning stimulates sufficient one-year-old wood, on which flowers are borne.

To ensure that the trees bear at a young age, and that they bear the finest of fruits, plant one of the named varieties. Among those most highly recommended are 'Sunflower', 'Overleese' and 'Taylor'.

JUNEBERRY

Juneberry (*Amelanchier* spp., Zones 3 to 8) is the common name for a group of native plants with uncommonly delicious fruits. The fruits look like blueberries but are sweet and juicy, with a flavor that has the richness of sweet cherry with a hint of almond. Only the few white-fruited varieties are not self-fruitful.

Species of juneberry grow wild everywhere in the United States and range from subshrubs to trees. Besides its delicious fruits, you may want to plant juneberry for its early spring show of pretty white or pinkish flowers, for its fiery autumn leaf color, or for its attractive, gray-striated bark, most appreciated in

A ripe American persimmon is as sweet as honey, with the texture and rich flavor of a wet, dried apricot. The tree grows wild in eastern woodlands.

winter. One species, known as the Saskatoon juneberry *(A. alnifolia),* is a large shrub that is planted both as an ornamental and, commercially, for its tasty, large berries. (I recently found one planted near an entrance to K-Mart.) While the tree species need little pruning, you should prune the bush species by cutting stems four or more years old to the ground to make way for new replacements.

AMERICAN PERSIMMON

American persimmon *(Diospyros virginiana,* Zones 5 to 8), another native fruit, has never been widely known or grown because it is too soft for commercial shipping. It has also gotten a bad rap from people who have bitten into unripe persimmons, which are extremely astringent. But softness is not a problem for fruits that need travel only as far as the fruit bowl. And a thoroughly ripened American persimmon is as sweet as honey, with the texture and rich flavor of a wet, dried apricot.

No one really understands the pollination needs of the American persimmon. Female trees sometimes need pollination, but sometimes bear fruits without pollination or bear a few male flowers that provide pollination. Some of the tastiest

Sprightly red currants make a beautiful jelly, but you also can let them hang on the bushes until dead ripe to eat fresh, right out in the garden.

varieties include 'Early Golden', 'Garretson' and 'Morris Burton'. In northern areas, plant varieties such as 'Meader', 'Hicks' and 'Szukis', which can survive bitterly cold winters and can ripen their fruits within a short growing season.

Persimmon is a handsome plant, a tree that grows large, but with drooping, bluish leaves, creates a relaxed, rather than imposing, appearance. Do not plant persimmon near driveways, walkways or terraces, where the falling fruit can create a mess. No need to prune your persimmon tree.

GOOSEBERRIES AND CURRANTS

The genus *Ribes* (Zones 3 to 5) includes both native and foreign species of gooseberries and currants. Europeans have always raved about these fruits, but they are just becoming better known here. Pop a fresh, ripe 'Whitesmith', 'Hinnonmaki Yellow' or 'Achilles' gooseberry into your mouth and you will understand why the flavor of the best gooseberries has been compared to that of the best grapes. Varieties of gooseberries differ not only in flavor, but also in appearance. Gooseberry color ranges from green to white and yellow to red and purple; fruit size ranges from as small as a pea to as large as a small plum.

Red currants are a sprightly fruit that makes a beautiful jelly, but you also can let them hang on the bushes until dead ripe to eat fresh, right out in the garden. White currants are identical to red currants, except that the fruits are white. Both fruits hang from the bushes in long clusters that look like strings of luminescent jewels. 'Red Lake' and 'Laxton's No. 1' are particularly tasty red varieties; 'White Versailles' and 'White Imperial' are good white ones.

Black currants are quite a different fruit from red or white currants, with a strong, resiny flavor that some people enjoy fresh, and everybody likes in juices, jams and tarts. Black currants also are extremely high in vitamin C. Where white pine blister rust disease is a threat, plant the rust-immune variety 'Consort'.

Despite the diversity of their fruits, cultivated *Ribes* prefer similar growing conditions. They are generally self-fruitful. Keep the ground beneath these bushes blanketed with a thick, organic mulch such as leaves or straw to keep the soil cool, moist and weed free. While the plants are dormant, prune to the ground any stems more than three years old from gooseberries and red currants; prune away two-year-old stems from black currants. Peeling or darkening bark on older stems makes them easy to distinguish from younger stems.

HARDY KIWI

One of the most delectable of uncommon fruits is the hardy kiwi *(Actinidia arguta,* Zones 4 to 7; *A. kolomikta,* Zones 3 to 7). As you can guess from the name, this fruit is a relative of the market kiwi. But unlike the market kiwi with its fuzzy skin and fruits the size of a large egg, the hardy kiwi has a smooth, edible skin and fruit the size of a grape. Inside, both fruits have the same emerald green flesh. But taste the hardy kiwi: It is a whit sweeter and more flavorful than the market kiwi. And the hardy kiwi, unlike the market kiwi, can be grown where winters are frigid.

Hardy kiwi plants are vigorous vines, many varieties of which are quite decorative with their red-stemmed or pink and white variegated leaves. Plant hardy kiwis to cover an arbor or pergola, allowing about 200 square feet per plant. Mostly, the plants are either male or female, so you need at least one male (nonfruiting) for up to eight females (which do fruit). Some good female varieties are 'Anna' ('Ananasnaja'), 'Issai' (not very hardy, but very precocious and partially self-fruitful), and 'Meader'. 'Meader Male' and 'Geneva Male' are good male pollinators.

Hardy kiwis do need annual pruning, twice each year. In summer, cut back any unruly stems. In winter, shorten stems that have fruited so that they are

Hardy kiwis are vigorous vines, and their red-stemmed or pink and white varie-gated leaves can be quite decorative.

Medlars are rock hard when harvested in autumn. Allow them to ripen indoors for a couple of weeks. They'll turn brown and mushy, but their flavor is superb, reminiscent of old-fashioned applesauce, spicy with winey overtones.

only 18 inches long and, occasionally, cut some all the way back to the permanent cordon to make way for new fruiting stems. Because males are needed only for their flowers, cut back their flowering shoots, to encourage new shoots, right after the plants bloom.

MEDLAR

Medlar *(Mespilus germanica)* is an uncommon fruit now, but was once widely enjoyed, reaching its peak of popularity in Europe during the Middle Ages. The downfall of this fruit has been its appearance: it looks like a small russeted apple with the calyx end (opposite the stem) flared open. Centuries ago, Chaucer called this the "open-arse" fruit. In this century, another writer aptly described the medlar as a "crabby-looking, brownish-green, truncated, little spheroid of unsympathetic appearance."

Medlars are rock hard when harvested in autumn. Before you can eat a medlar, you must allow it to ripen indoors for a couple of weeks or more, during which time the flesh turns brown and mushy. Despite the fruit's unappetizing appearance, the flavor is superb, reminiscent of old-fashioned applesauce, spicy with winey overtones.

The medlar plant is a small tree, which itself is not at all ugly. The flowers look like wild roses, and appear in late spring cradled in whorls of leaves. In autumn, the foliage turns warm shades of yellow, orange and russet. Medlars are self-fruitful. Among the best varieties are 'Nottingham' and 'Giant' (also called 'Dutch' or 'Dutch Giant').

Above: The ornamental jujube tree needs a long growing season. When ripe (left), the plum-sized fruit has crisp, sweet flesh. With further ripening the jujube dries and sweetens.

JUJUBE

Jujube *(Ziziphus jujuba,* Zones 5 to 10), is uncommon here, but grows in abundance in Asia, its native home: Until recently, there were more jujube trees than any other type of fruit tree in China. As this plum-sized fruit first ripens, the skin looks like mahogany that has been buffed smooth and shiny; the flesh within is crisp and sweet, reminiscent of apple. Let the fruits ripen longer, and they live up to their other common name, "Chinese dates," as the skins begin to shrivel, and the flesh darkens, dries and sweetens.

Jujube is a small tree with glossy little leaves, and has been extensively planted in the southern tier of the United States, usually as an ornamental. This is a cosmopolitan tree, tolerating searing summers as well as frigid winters, and dry as well as waterlogged soils. What the jujube does need is to be bathed in sunlight and a growing season long enough to ripen the fruits.

The pollination needs of the jujube are not clear. Some varieties are allegedly self-fertile, possibly depending on climate. But even self-fertile varieties set more and larger fruit with cross-pollination. Two of the best and most readily available varieties are 'Li' and 'Lang'. And yes, candied jujube fruits were the original jujube candy.

And so ends this sampler of uncommon fruits. Remember it is only a sampler; the list could go on to include gumi, raisin tree, edible honeysuckle, highbush cranberry and more. I predict that many of these newly discovered fruits—or, rather, rediscovered fruits—with their delectable flavors, will not be uncommon for long.

89

ORNAMENTAL FRUITS

Pleasing the Eye & the Mouth

BY ROBERT KOURIK

THE BEAUTY OF ORNAMENTAL EDIBLES is in the eye and the mouth of the beholder—and the goal of the fruit gardener is to satisfy both. Sometimes this aim can be achieved with an ordinary 'Yellow Delicious' apple tree with its fountain of white springtime blooms. A more impressive display, however, comes with an unusual apple variety like 'Pink Pearl', whose blossoms are streaked a delightful hot-pink. And 'Pink Pearl' fruit is not ho-hum: The medium-crisp hot-pink-and-white marbled flesh is firm enough for baking and has a delightful sweet-tart flavor. 'Pink Pearl' represents the hedonistic marriage of beauty and flavor.

The search for fruits that are both tasty and ornamental is beset with pitfalls. Some "edible" ornamentals, such as wild gooseberries native to the West *(Ribes sanguineum,* for example) are unproductive, and any fruit produced tastes bland. Other superior-flavored edibles offer no dramatic visual impact. 'Seckel' pear has an exquisite, sweet-spicy flavor and a buttery texture, but the appearance of the fruit, the fall color of the leaves and the shape of the tree are just ordinary. Here, a gardener would choose a 'Seckel' pear for its gourmet value over its visual impact in the garden.

Like children, all plants are beautiful to someone. But here are some important guidelines as to what's commonly considered "ornamental:"

Top: Brightly or complexly colored
fruits satisfy the eye.
Right: With a little effort, you can train
a fruit tree into an interesting shape.

- Shiny, glossy leaves with a rich green or unusual foliage color
- Interesting bark
- With deciduous plants, dramatic fall color
- Showy, colorful or unusual flowers
- Fruit brightly colored or with a complex blush
- Interesting or unusually shaped fruit
- Neat or interesting growth habit

Still, practicality should always be a major concern in the food garden. Many handsome subtropical plants bear tasty fruits, but their requirements—a greenhouse, seasonal covering or heaters—limit their wide-

An edible hedge in bloom—Nanking cherry, juneberry and European black currant.

Espaliered apples ornament a property's perimeter.

spread use as ornamental edibles. Similarly, if rigorous pest control or hand-pollination is required to get a decent crop of any fruit, the practical limitations may outweigh the harvest's value. Be sure to check a plant's susceptibility to pests and diseases with your local Cooperative Extension, especially in the eastern half of the country, which has more than its share of pest problems.

Also consider the tree's fruiting capacity. Some relatively pest-free trees, such as quince and American and Oriental persimmon, might bear too abundantly for your taste. Are you going to be able to deal with countless pints of jelly? Most people feel guilty if fruit rots, so pick a fruit for which you have plenty of use and lots of recipes.

Think carefully about where you plant. Fallen fruit can be unsafe and stain concrete or wood. Some fruits fall easily when ripe and are very messy, so should not be planted near sidewalks, patios, driveways and decks. Untidy fruits include persimmon, mulberry, pear, apple, peach and nectarine. Fruits such as grape, quince, kiwi, jujube and Cornelian cherry cling longer to the plant, or have firm skins.

What follows is a list of some fruits that are borne on attractive, relatively easy-to-cultivate plants that grow well over a wide range and are relatively pest free.

Alpine strawberry *(Fragaria vesca):* Dainty flowers and fruits are produced throughout the growing season from these runnerless plants. Fruits are very aromatic, with a hint of pineapple in white-fruited varieties. Alpine strawberries are self-fruitful and thrive in Zones 3 to 10, in sun or part shade and well-drained soil.

Blueberry *(Vaccinium angustifolium, V. corymbosum, V. ashei):* See page 54.

Cornelian cherry *(Cornus mas):* This petite tree is covered with small yellow blossoms in late winter or very early spring, red "cherries" in summer and mahogany-colored leaves in fall. The fruits are tart. While not absolutely necessary for fruiting, cross-pollination increases yields. Cornelian cherry grows well in Zones 3 to 8, and needs full sun.

Highbush cranberry *(Viburnum trilobum):* This large bush is covered with flat clusters of sparkling white flowers in spring, then red fruits in late summer. The berries, which persist well into winter, are not true cranberries, but can be cooked in the same way to make jellies and sauces. Plant from Zones 2 to 7, in full sun and well-drained soil.

Jujube *(Ziziphus jujuba):* See page 89.

Kiwi *(Actinidia* spp.*):* See page 86.

Lingonberry *(Vaccinium vitis-idaea):* This small shrub is related to the true cranberry, and bears a similar fruit. Like cranberry, lingonberry spreads over

The blossoms of the apple 'Pink Pearl' are streaked a delightful hot pink, and the fruit has pink-and-white marbled flesh—a hedonistic marriage of beauty and flavor.

the ground, sending out under-ground shoots. The leaves are glossy like those of holly, but daintier and not spined. There are two botanical species; plants of the smaller one, var. *minus,* grow but a few inches high and have leaves only 1/4- to 1/2-inch long. Plant lingonberry in Zones 2 to 6, in full sun or partial shade (the latter where summers are hot). The soil must be very acidic, well-drained and rich in organic matter.

Medlar *(Mespilus germanica):* See page 88.

Nanking cherry *(Prunus tomentosa):* This large bush is drenched in

Top: 'Pink Panda' strawberries will put some pizzazz into your strawberry bed.
Above: 'Pink Pearl' apples are firm enough for baking and have a sweet-tart flavor.

95

Left: These white grapes, with striking foliage and beautiful fruit clusters, meet all the requirements of the ornamental edible. Bottom: Quince trees bear large, golden, fuzzy fruits after a late spring showing of white blossoms resembling wild roses.

In the spring, the highbush cranberry (not a true cranberry) is covered with clusters of sparkling white flowers. Then in late summer its red berries appear, remaining on the bush into winter.

pinkish white flowers in early spring. With cross-pollination, the bush is likewise drenched in red cherries by early summer. The fruit is a true cherry with a slightly tart flavor that varies somewhat from plant to plant. Some varieties bear pale yellow instead of red fruit. The plant tolerates bitter winter cold, scathing summer heat and drought. Nanking cherry grows well in Zones 3 to 6, in full sun and well-drained soil.

Pawpaw *(Asimina triloba):* See page 82.

Persimmon *(Diospyros kaki, D. virginiana):* The American persimmon is described on page 84. The kaki, or Oriental persimmon, is a similar tree, except that it is generally suited to Zones 7 to 10, and its fruits are larger and juicier. You can eat so-called nonastringent kakis when they are fully colored and still crisp. Nonastringent kakis need hot summer weather, and some can be eaten when the flesh is still firm only if pollinated. Wait to eat so-called astringent kakis when they are fully colored and as soft as jelly.

Quince *(Cydonia oblonga):* Quince grows as a small tree with a single trunk or as a multistemmed bush. White or pink blossoms that resemble those of wild roses appear in late spring. The fruits that follow the flowers also are ornamental—they're large, yellow and fuzzy. They are inedible raw, but make a fine jelly and add pizzazz to an apple pie. Plant quince from Zones 5 to 9, in full sun and well-drained soil.

Bud-grafting: Insertion of a single bud of a scion under the bark on a rootstock plant. Sometime after grafting, the trunk is cut close to the new bud, and the scion becomes the fruiting part of the tree.

Central leader tree: A tree form in which the central axis of the tree is a continuation of the trunk, off which grow scaffold limbs.

Chill hours: Number of hours temperate-zone plants must have at about 32° to 45° F during their dormant period in order to flower in the spring.

Cordon: A woody plant grown as a single permanent stem or permanent extension off the main trunk from which fruiting canes grow.

Cross pollination: Transfer of pollen from one fruit variety to another variety of the same fruit.

Feathered tree: A young nursery-grown tree with branches.

Fruit set: Completion of the fertilization process, evidenced by a swelling of the ovary.

Genetic dwarf variety: A fruit plant that is a dwarf as a result of its own genetic structure rather than the genetic makeup of its rootstock.

Graft union: The place where rootstock and scion join, indicated by a slight swelling, change of bark color or slight bend in the trunk.

Interspecific hybrid: A plant derived from the crossing of more than one species.

Open center tree: A tree form with three to five scaffold limbs growing upward and outward atop a short trunk, creating a vase shape.

Rootstock: The portion of the tree that includes the roots and lower part of the trunk, onto which the scion is grafted.

Scion: A branch or bud of a desired variety that is grafted onto a rootstock, and which subsequently gives rise to the fruiting portion of the tree.

Scaffold limb: The main structural branch of the tree.

Self-fruitful (Self-fertile): Plants that are capable of fertilizing their flowers with their own pollen.

Spur: A short, permanent stem on which fruit is borne.

Water sprout: A very vigorous, vertical shoot growing from the branch of a tree.

Whip: A young nursery-grown tree consisting of a single, unbranched stem.

NURSERY SOURCES

BRITTINGHAM PLANT FARMS
P.O. Box 2538
Salisbury, MD 21802
410-742-1594

BURNT RIDGE NURSERY
432 Burnt Ridge Rd.
Onalaska, WA 98570
206-985-2873

DEGRANDCHAMP'S BLUEBERRY FARM
15576 77th St.
South Haven, MI 49090
616-637-3915

EDIBLE LANDSCAPING
P.O. Box 77
Afton, VA 22920
800-524-4156

FEDCO TREES
P.O. Box 520
Waterville, ME 04903
207-873-7333

FOWLER GARDEN CENTER & NURSERIES
525 Fowler Rd.
Newcastle, CA 95658
916-645-8191

HARMONY FARM SUPPLY
P.O. Box 460
Graton, CA 95444
707-823-9125

HARTMANN'S PLANTATION
P.O. Box E
310 60th St.
Grand Junction, MI 49056
616-252-4281

HIDDEN SPRINGS NURSERY
170 Hidden Springs Ln.
Cookeville, TN 38501
615-268-9889

JOHNSON NURSERY
Rte. 5, Box 29J
Ellijay, GA 30540
706-276-3187

LAWSON'S NURSERY
2730 Yellow Creek Rd.
Ball Ground, GA 30107
770-893-2141

LOUISIANA NURSERY
Rte. 7, Box 43
Opelousas, LA 70570
318-948-3696

PLUMTREE NURSERY
387 Springtown Rd.
New Paltz, NY 12561
914-255-0417

MELLINGER'S
2310 West South Range Rd.
North Lima, OH 44452
216-549-9861

RAINTREE NURSERY
391 Butts Rd.
Morton, WA 98356
360-496-6400

NORTH STAR GARDENS
2124 University Ave W.
St. Paul, MN 55114-1838
612-227-9842

ROCKY MEADOW ORCHARD & NURSERY
360 Rocky Meadow NW
New Salisbury, IN 47161
812-347-2213

NORTHWOODS NURSERY
27635 S. Oglesby Rd.
Canby, OR 97013
503-266-5432

SOUTHMEADOW FRUIT GARDENS
Cleveland Ave. 10603
Baroda, MI 49116
616-422-2411

NOURSE FARMS INC
41 River Road
South Deerfield, MA 01373
413-665-2658

STARK BROTHERS
P.O. Box 10
Louisiana, MO 63353-0010
314-754-5511

OREGON EXOTIC RARE FRUIT NURSERY
1065 Messenger Rd.
Grants Pass, OR 97527
503-846-7578

TRIPPLE BROOK FARM
37 Middle Rd.
Southampton, MA 01073
413-527-4626

FURTHER READING

THE BACKYARD ORCHARDIST
Stella Otto
Ottographics, 1993

THE BACKYARD BERRY BOOK
Stella Otto
Ottographics, 1995

FRUIT IN THE GARDEN
Norman Taylor
Van Nostrand, 1954

UNCOMMON FRUITS WORTHY OF ATTENTION: A GARDENER'S GUIDE
Lee Reich
Addison-Wesley Publishing, 1991

THE ORGANIC GARDENER'S HANDBOOK OF NATURAL INSECT AND DISEASE CONTROL
Barbara Ellis and Fern Bradley (eds.)
Rodale Press, 1992

HARDINESS ZONES

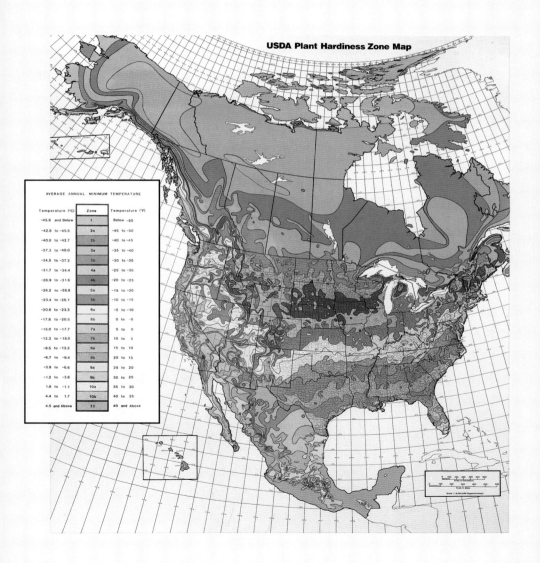

USDA Plant Hardiness Zone Map

AVERAGE ANNUAL MINIMUM TEMPERATURE

Temperature (°C)	Zone	Temperature (°F)
-45.6 and Below	1	Below -50
-42.8 to -45.5	2a	-45 to -50
-40.0 to -42.7	2b	-40 to -45
-37.3 to -40.0	3a	-35 to -40
-34.5 to -37.2	3b	-30 to -35
-31.7 to -34.4	4a	-25 to -30
-28.9 to -31.6	4b	-20 to -25
-26.2 to -28.8	5a	-15 to -20
-23.4 to -26.1	5b	-10 to -15
-20.6 to -23.3	6a	-5 to -10
-17.8 to -20.5	6b	0 to -5
-15.0 to -17.7	7a	5 to 0
-12.3 to -15.0	7b	10 to 5
-9.5 to -12.2	8a	15 to 10
-6.7 to -9.4	8b	20 to 15
-3.9 to -6.6	9a	25 to 20
-1.2 to -3.8	9b	30 to 25
1.6 to -1.1	10a	35 to 30
4.4 to 1.7	10b	40 to 35
4.5 and Above	11	40 and Above

CONTRIBUTORS

LEE REICH is devoted to fruits both as a vocation and avocation. He earned his doctorate in horticulture at the University of Maryland, and since retiring from fruit research at Cornell University has been a horticultural consultant and writer. In addition to magazine and newspaper articles, his books include *Uncommon Fruits Worthy of Attention* (1991), *A Northeast Gardener's Year* (1992) and *The Joy of Pruning* (1996). He also has an extensive planting of backyard fruits—both common and uncommon varieties.

DAVID CAIN is vice president of research and development for Sun World, a company that grows and markets more than 75 fruits and vegetables. He is responsible for coordinating the company's plant breeding programs and developing new varieties. Before joining Superior Farming Company in 1986, which was acquired by Sun World, he was a research scientist at the U.S. Department of Agriculture for nine years.

ED FACKLER is the owner and manager of Rocky Meadow Orchard and Nursery in New Salisbury, Indiana. He and his family maintain one of the largest private collections of apple and pear varieties in the world. He has lectured throughout the country on various aspects of fruit growing, including his seven years of experience with organic fruit culture and thirteen years of experience in common-sense control of fruit pests.

DANIEL HARTMANN is vice president and general manager of Hartmann's Plantation Inc., a family business that has been raising blueberry plants and fruits for 52 years. Daniel began working with his father in the business when he was 12 years old, and has been in the blueberry plant and fruit business for the past three decades.

ROBERT KOURIK is the author and publisher of *Designing and Maintaining Your Edible Landscape—Naturally,* and of two other titles from Metamorphic Press. He is currently publishing "Bob's Honest to Goodness Newsletter."

PAUL M. OTTEN has worked with berries for over four decades. He has been the president and executive secretary of the North American Bramble Growers Association and on the board of three other professional grower associations. In the early 1980s, he established North Star Gardens, a Minnesota nursery specializing in berry plants. He consults, lectures and writes on berries, and edits and publishes *Northland Berry News*, a quarterly newsletter-magazine.

MARVIN P. PRITTS is a professor and researcher at Cornell University specializing in strawberries, raspberries, blueberries and other small fruits. He is also research chairperson of the North American Strawberry Growers Association and on the advisory board of the New York State Berry Growers Association.

SALLY ROTH, a lifelong naturalist and gardener, is a contributing editor of *Fine Gardening* magazine and a nature and gardening columnist for the *Courier* in Evansville, Indiana. She and her family live in New Harmony, Indiana, where they publish *A Letter from the Country,* a bimonthly nature journal.

LON J. ROMBOUGH is an Oregon-based researcher and consultant who locates and develops new or uncommon varieties and species of fruits and nuts for a range of clients from individuals to companies. He has also published articles on new and unusual fruits and nuts in *Horticulture, Fine Gardening* and *Organic Gardening*.

ILLUSTRATION CREDITS

INDEX

Gardening Books for the Next Century from the Brooklyn Botanic Garden

Don't miss any of the gardening books in Brooklyn Botanic Garden's 21st-Century Gardening Series! Published four times a year, these acclaimed books explore the frontiers of ecological gardening—offering practical, step-by-step tips on creating environmentally sensitive and beautiful gardens for the 1990s and the new century. Your subscription to BBG's 21st-Century Gardening Series is free with Brooklyn Botanic Garden membership.

To become a member, please call (718) 622-4433, ext. 265. Or photocopy this form, complete and return to: Membership Department, Brooklyn Botanic Garden, 1000 Washington Avenue, Brooklyn, NY 11225-1099.

SUBSCRIPTIONS

Your name ....

Address ....

City/State/Zip ....Phone ....

AMOUNT

☐ Yes, I want to subscribe to the 21st-Century Gardening Series (4 quarterly volumes) by becoming a member of the Brooklyn Botanic Garden:

☐ $35 (Subscriber)   ☐ $125 (Signature Member)

☐ $50 (Partner)   ☐ $300 (Benefactor)   ....

☐ Enclosed is my tax-deductible contribution to the Brooklyn Botanic Garden.   ....

TOTAL   ....

Form of payment: ☐ Check enclosed ☐ Visa ☐ Mastercard

Credit card# ....Exp ....

Signature ....

FOR INFORMATION ON ORDERING ANY OF THE FOLLOWING BACK TITLES, PLEASE WRITE THE BROOKLYN BOTANIC GARDEN AT THE ABOVE ADDRESS OR CALL (718) 622-4433, EXT. 274.

American Cottage Gardening
Annuals: A Gardener's Guide
Bonsai: Special Techniques
Butterfly Gardens
Culinary Herbs
Easy-care Roses
The Environmental Gardener
Ferns
Garden Photography
The Gardener's World of Bulbs
Gardening for Fragrance
Gardening in the Shade
Gardening with Wildflowers
  & Native Plants

Going Native: Biodiversity
  in Our Own Backyards
Greenhouses & Garden Rooms
Herbs & Cooking
Herbs & Their Ornamental Uses
Hollies: A Gardener's Guide
Indoor Bonsai
Japanese Gardens
Native Perennials
The Natural Lawn & Alternatives
Natural Insect Control
A New Look at Vegetables
A New Look at Houseplants
Orchids for the Home

  & Greenhouse
Ornamental Grasses
Perennials: A Gardener's Guide
Pruning Techniques
Roses
Salad Gardens
Shrubs: The New Glamour Plants
Soils
The Town & City Gardener
Trees: A Gardener's Guide
Water Gardening
The Winter Garden
Woodland Gardens: Shade
  Gets Chic